YOUNG AT HEART

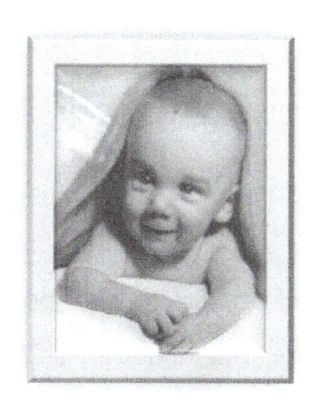

Randolph, Radio and the Road to Retirement

Steve Yanofsky

Foreword by Mike Morin

FOREWORD

Mike Morin
51-year radio and TV personality
Author, columnist, speaker, bread baker

 Congratulations to Steve Young/Yanofsky, newest inductee into my newly-created Happy Life Hall of Fame. To be nominated, one must have lived a life of gratification and purpose while remaining generous and humble. He has.

Steve has it all; a wonderful wife, Paula, and a fabulous son, Daniel. Along with a successful career and countless friends, would he have traded all that to play power forward for the Boston Celtics? Close, but doubtful, as he'd only be happy about every 20 years since 1986, instead of enjoying his daily happiness now. Steve loves all things sports and enjoys sharing his views on the topic.

My 35-year friendship with Steve began when he joined the staff of Curt Gowdy Broadcasting's radio stations WCGY FM and WCCM AM in suburban Boston, just a few months after I joined as WCGY morning host in 1986. WCGY 93.7 was on the cusp of regional prominence and marketing whiz Steve Young was there to advance station billing and visibility.

Steve was a one man promotions machine. He created effective ad campaigns and stayed involved all through the process. He carved an invaluable niche for himself by documenting station events and promotions with his video camera. His gracious personality brought out the best in his video subjects.

Steve organized and managed the WCGY Rock Sox staff softball team that turned out to be the social heartbeat of the stations. He was in his glory when the Rock Sox played fundraiser games against the Boston Bruins and another that featured local Cy Young pitcher Steve Bedrosian. Steve Young could very well be Cy Young's brother, save for the obvious age difference. The elder Young had mad baseball pitching skills. The junior Young spun enviable sales pitches. Both worthy of Hall of Fame accolades.

The Happy Life Hall of Fame welcomes Steve Young/Yanofsky. He never got to play on the Boston Garden parquet professionally but he enjoyed a wonderful life and stellar career and will always be surrounded by the many who love him.

Mike Morin, 2021

PROLOGUE AND DEDICATION

Why write an autobiography? Now retired, I found myself with more time to examine what events and life stories have gotten me to this point. Writing forces me to think and rethink my past and my present, the people around me and the relationships that seemed ordinary at the time, but truly has made my life extraordinary. I don't want those details to be forgotten or altered over the course of time.

My book was completed in 2021. Now in my late 60's, the line between fact and memory start to fade. Sometimes I can't remember what I did 10 minutes ago, let alone 60 years ago. Writing this book has allowed me to present my side of the story, as well as my interpretation of facts, in a way in which I can communicate my triumphs, joys and disappointments.

I read a story about a father who had written his autobiography and how his son will always remember him as a good husband, father and friend. It gave his son great comfort that his father put pen to paper and that there was now concrete evidence for him, his family and generations of people to follow. His father used to say, "We come into and go out of this world alone, but the quality of our lives depends upon the people we touch along the way. It is the stories of love that remind us who we are and why we are here."

It is my intent to honor the ones that I love and so many of the relationships I cherished. Maybe I look at it as a time capsule of my life, the opportunity to share these memories with my family, friends and to those who do not know me quite as well. This is an account of many of my life experiences and I hope you enjoy reading them. I feel that through the years I've developed so many special relationships that have given me purpose. The end result... lots of love and the feeling that just maybe I did matter to those that crossed my path.

Why *Young at Heart*? The title comes from the popular Sinatra ballad published in 1953, ironically the year I was born. My love of Sinatra's music started at a very early age. Growing up in the projects of Dorchester, Massachusetts in the late 50's and early 60's, my mom and dad played his music all the time on the record player, whether they were 45's or albums. Later in life, my dad and I would croon the tunes together at family gatherings. To this day, when I visit my Dad's gravesite, I'll sing a few of his favorite tunes, normally with the birds in the trees as my enchanted and chirpy audience. There was one particular visit that happened in late November that was nothing short of bizarre and a bit eerie. The trees were bare, winter was fast approaching and there were no birds in sight. I'm sure by now they all had flown south for the winter. My plan during this particular visit was to do a little maintenance work around the area and when that was completed, tell Dad what's been going on with Ma and the rest of the family. After the mini-speech, I proceeded to sing a few of his favorite Sinatra tunes. I selected "Where or When," and then followed it up with "That's Life."

When I began the private concert a very strange thing happened. A huge flock of birds came out of nowhere and chirped away as loudly as you can imagine. I'm talking about a couple of hundred birds, at least. I was a bit taken aback. I stared at this incredible sight and of course thought that it was a sign that my Dad heard everything I was saying and singing. I continued "That's Life" while staring up to the heavens. Then in a flash when the song came to its conclusion, the birds flew away as fast as they came. Strange but true.

Lou Yanofsky was always "Young at Heart" and I've heard from many that I'm pretty much a carbon copy of my beloved old man. I might be in my late 60's, but always try my best to act like I'm in my 30's. It keeps me young, I think. If you ask my wife, Paula, she'll tell you that I act more like I'm 10 years old. In retirement, my goal is to continue being young at heart. Stay active, ride my bike, go out for dinner with family and friends, keep in touch with former co-workers, play basketball, go to concerts, celebrate the holidays, visit my mother and keep on singing. I've learned that when I sing, I'm usually having a good day! With that said, I'm exhausted thinking about the things that I just mentioned. Being retired is a lot of work.

I dedicate this book to my dad, who passed away at the age of 87 in 2012, and to my mother, Jacqui, who turned the big 9-0 in 2020. They both taught me to love family, be a good person, work hard and treat people the way you would like to be treated.

I also dedicate this book to my incredible wife, Paula, and my wonderful son, Daniel, a real mensch. They've listened and lived these stories far too often. I know that someday soon I better get new material. For the purpose of this book, I may already have all the material I need.

Young at Heart is based on the wonderful people I've encountered along the way and the priceless relationships that have been formed. After all, aren't the relationships you've developed throughout your life what it's all about?

Writing a book is a major undertaking and I want to thank several people for their help and inspiration. When I started writing the book, I turned to Mike Morin, the host of "Morin in the Morning," who I worked with at WCGY/WCCM in Lawrence in the late 80's and early 90's. Mike was a very successful and talented on-air personality for many years, a good friend and an author of several books. He was also quite the pitcher when it came to our company softball team! Mike encouraged me to continue to write and follow my passion. I really appreciated his advice.

Finally, I'd like to thank my three favorite sportswriters. Throughout my life as a sports geek, I've been an avid reader of the *Boston Globe's* sports pages. Bob Ryan, Jackie MacMullan and Dan Shaughnessy are my three favorite writers. All three are award-winning authors and I've always referred to them as my own personal BIG THREE. They inspired me to write. I've had the good fortune to meet them and in some cases work with them as well.

To write a book has been a lifelong dream. It was important to me to put pen to the paper as I start to close in on turning 70. My radio career began in 1977, but I'd also like to share with you the stories leading up to that time. It chronicles my life from my upbringing in Dorchester and Randolph to my seven radio 'families' and the personal memorable events that took place along the way. This book is about the people and the stories that helped to shape my life. From interviewing sports celebs, serving as a play-by-play announcer for two college basketball teams. and working four decades as a sales manager/account exec, it all added up to one amazing journey. I don't regret a single moment.

Forty-one years in radio, seven radio stations, hundreds of incredible co-workers and now three years into retirement. ...it's time to fulfill the dream. I hope you enjoy my book.

"If you should survive till 105, think of all you'll derive from being alive. And here is the best part, you'll have a head start, if you are amongst the very young at heart."
Frank Sinatra/music by
Johny Richards/lyrics by Carolyn Leigh

TABLE OF CONTENTS

Foreword by Mike Morin ... 2

Prologue and Dedication ... 4

Chapter One ... 15

Dorchest-ah Days with a Splash of Mattapan

Chapter Two ... 36

Entering Randolph:

Taffy Apples, the RBA, 100-yard Dash and the Invisible Jukebox

Chapter Three ... 47

College Days:

The Draft, Fenway's Bleachers and An Attempt at Love

Chapter Four ... 58

Radio: In the Beginning

Chapter Five ... 73

Moving on Up to the Queen City

Chapter Six … 79

Homeowners Twice Over

Chapter Seven … 82

Working for a Legend in Lawrence, Two More Fathers, Two More Radio Stations

Chapter Eight … 99

WSSH-ing to Make a Lot of Dough

Chapter Nine … 104

W-R-O-R: Wish I Could Pronounce My 'R's

Chapter Ten … 112

14 Years of Rollin' on the River

Chapter Eleven … 144

Valley 98.9, the Final Radio Station, Finally Benefits of Retirement

Chapter Twelve ... 150
The Life of a Sports Geek
- Sports Shorts
- Boston Marathon 2013
- Jack Thornton
- Remembering my first game at Fenway
- A secret undercover mission
- Moses reviews the East Coast Baseball League draft

Chapter Thirteen ... 181
Pieces of Poetry, Randomly Speaking
- Brady at the Snap
- Twas the night before Passover
- Snow
- A Day to Remember
- Life in Heaven, a tribute to my dad

Chapter Fourteen ... 190
Picture My Family

Chapter Fifteen ... 211
Dad 's Behind the Eight Ball

Chapter Sixteen ... 214

Merry and Daniel and a Couple of Cool Cats
- Wedding of the Century
- With Two Cats in the Yard
- Travel Agents Extraordinaire

Chapter Seventeen ... 230

Jacqui, Jacqueline, Jackie and Ma

Chapter Eighteen ... 233

Good Friends are Hard to Find Unless You Meet Them in High School

Chapter Nineteen ... 242

Tribute to Bernie, Stairway to Heaven by Daniel Yanofsky

Chapter Twenty ... 245

List of Favorites

Chapter Twenty-One ... 248

In Memoriam

Chapter Twenty-Two ... 252
Saving the Best for Last

Chapter Twenty-Three ... 255
Parting Shots

CHAPTER ONE

Dorchest-ah Days with a Splash of Mattapan

In the beginning....

The multi-talented Billy Crystal once toured the country with an incredible one-man show called "700 Sundays." Crystal strutted around the stage reviewing his life with an array of pictures and videos in the background. Filled with emotion and never-ending comedy, this was undoubtedly Billy Crystal at his best. While he recalled, so vividly, his family memories, I was overwhelmed by the feeling that I was inadequate because I couldn't remember many of the moments that I experienced as a child. I'm sure that Crystal embellished his stories for entertainment purposes, but why couldn't I remember more?

So, I thought to myself, if I write what I do remember, I'll feel better. Not that I'm about to go on tour like Crystal, but the memories will survive on these very pages.

I was born in 1953. Of course, I don't remember too much about living in the 50's. Never once did I pick up my daily newspaper and see a 1950's dateline. My parents, Jacqui and Lou, certainly took enough pictures, so I do have tangible proof that I was there. To learn a little bit more about 1953, I did some research and found these interesting facts and figures.

* *TV Guide* debuts and on the cover of the first issue were Lucille Ball and her newborn son, Desi Arnaz Jr. In fact, Lucy appeared on the *TV Guide* cover 39 times, more than anyone else. And you thought that this book would only be about me? You learn something new every day...

* The US Supreme Court rules by a 7-2 count that baseball is a sport not a business. Huh???

* The first color TV sets appear and sells for $1,175. Transistor radios also debuted in 1953

* Top-rated TV shows: *I Love Lucy* (seems to be a theme here) *Dragnet* and *You Bet Your Life*. Other popular shows included *Make Room for Daddy* with Danny Thomas, *GE Theatre*, *Twenty Questions* and *the Red Skelton Show*.

* *Peter Pan* was released

* Top-selling book was *Casino Royale* by Ian Fleming

* Celebrities born in 1953: Pierce Brosnan, Tim Allen and Hulk Hogan

*Average cost of a car: Under $4,000.

*Gallon of gas: 2 cents.

*Average income: $4,011.

*Average cost of a home: $8,200.

*Postage stamp: 3 cents.

When it came to the late 50's, I certainly remember growing up in the projects of Dorchester, Massachusetts. One Ames Street to be exact, across the street from Franklin Field. My brother, Ken, who is four years younger than me, along with my parents, lived on the first floor of a three-decker orange brick building. My dad worked at the Watertown Arsenal in the printing department. Several years later it was converted to the United States Army Materials and Mechanics Research Center. He also worked at a local toy store called Hobby Fair on Blue Hill Avenue in Mattapan Square. We never had a lot of money, but always seemed to make ends meet. My mother, Jackie, was the perfect Jewish mother. From caring to worrying and being the ultimate cook and baker, my brother and I were never denied anything. Let the truth be told. My mother changed the spelling of her name to Jacqui after being inspired following a trip to France! More on my parents later in this book.

My memories of Dorchester included playing marbles, red rover, tag, whiffle ball, flipping baseball cards and going to school. I thought that it was quite a schlep to walk from One Ames Street to the Bradford School, but after further review it was less than a two-mile jaunt.

Me, Alan Bahn and Jonathan Frank getting ready to play ball, circa 1960

My cousin Elaine was also a big part of my life. According to my mother's all-inclusive baby book, I referred to cousin Elaine as E-yarn. She spent countless hours playing with me and reliable sources say that I always looked forward to her visits. Her brother, Michael, was also a big part of our family and later on became an accomplished drummer. Another person that deserves special credit is my great-grandmother, Dora, or more affectionately known as 'Grandma.'

She was my number one baby sitter and I adored her. Grandma gave me all her love and attention during my early care-free years and I'll never forget her never-ending devotion and love towards me.

Sometimes I think of our Dorchester family of friends as the Little Rascals. We had a diverse mix of friendly characters that all came together in the projects. We lived on the first floor, the Bahn's on the second and the Frank's on the third. I was close to both families; Carol, Joyce and Alan Bahn and their parents Sarah and Joe, the Frank family, Natalie and Sumner and their children Jonathan, Jamie, Andrea and Claudia. The picture above includes the Gerber family, Carol and Alan Bahn and Kenny and I. Looks like I always took care of my little brother!

Earlier, I mentioned flipping baseball cards. The premise was to flip the cards against the wall of our building. The person who flipped their cards closet to the wall would win their opponents' cards. In addition, if you 'kissed' the cards (landed on top of your opponent's cards) you'd collect both cards. I'll never forget it. It was Sunday and it was time to try to win cards to add to my precious baseball collection. Unfortunately, I had a bad cold. Luckily I found the perfect fill-in....my dad! He volunteered to take my spot and challenge my buddies. I gave him one hundred cards and begged him not to lose. Well, about an hour later, he came home and made a bee-line towards my bedroom. I was still under the weather and was covered from head to toe with two heavy blankets. With a smirk on his face, followed by an evil smile, he proceeded to spill a batch of baseball cards onto my bed. I noticed pretty quickly that there weren't 100 baseball cards that I entrusted him with. As I counted the cards, my father smiled like a child who just had ice cream for the first time, still he didn't say a word. It took me awhile, but the final tally became official. My new baseball card collection grew to 300! He tripled the amount! What a dad!!! I felt much better at that moment. Then all of a sudden it crossed my mind that my dear old dad had taken my Little

Rascal friends to the cleaners. How would I face them ever again? I was very lucky the next day. Not only did my cold disappear but the Baseball Card Gods were smiling down upon me. My friends came over to play and never said a word. About 50 years later he would do something similar, this time playing billiards. But that's a story for another page.

Speaking of baseball cards, I remember that there was nothing better than going to a local candy store called Waldman's and dishing out 10 cents (money from my parents and my grandmother, known as 'Nanny') and opening a brand new deck of cards. As a bonus, the pack of cards included a stick of bubble gum. It didn't get much better than that! By the way, the baseball card that made me most happy was my all-time favorite, the "Say Hey Kid," Willie Mays of the San Francisco Giants. I read recently that a Willie Mays card today in mint condition sells for $93,412! Wonder if that was his rookie card. Unfortunately, after all the flipping of my cards on the hard black-tarred pavement, none of my baseball cards would have qualified as being "mint."

Another childhood memory was the purchase of my first pet. While others bought cats and dogs, my first pet was a tiny baby turtle. This major purchase was made at Woolworth's 5&10 on Blue Hill Avenue. The sales clerk showed me and my mother his last remaining turtle in-stock. 300 baseball cards and now my very own turtle! This was nirvana to me as a seven year old. I took the turtle home, played with him for a couple of hours and then noticed that the turtle was not moving at all. I asked my bewildered mother, "What's wrong with baby turtle?" She didn't mince words. "The turtle is dead." This was devastating news. My mother took me back to the store where we purchased the yet-to-be named turtle or in this case, the never-to-be-named turtle. We spoke to the clerk who sold me the damaged goods. He looked me square in the eyes and said, "What did you think you'd get for a nickel?" After that traumatic incident, I decided to stick to baseball cards. I never bought another pet again.

I remember going to school in 1960. Thinking back, things were quite different then. There were no school buses, no cafeteria and no gymnasium. We ate lunch at our iron-clad desks, nailed into the floor. As it turns out, 1960 was a stressful time for me. Not too long after losing my first pet, my next episode occurred soon after. During first grade recess, the class was playing tag. I was chasing classmate Joey Finkelstein and tagged him rather aggressively (I suppose) and ripped his shirt off his back. It must've been made of cheap material. I was frightened and proceeded to offer Joey pads and pads of colorful paper in exchange for his silence. I knew I could get the pads of paper from my father's workplace. Finkelstein didn't take the bait or bribe and I was summoned to appear in front of the third grade tribunal led by the wicked witch of the school and its principal, Miss O'Hearn.

There was an inside rumor that bad boys would be punished and tortured by Miss O'Hearn with a device called "the rat hand." Word had spread that Miss O'Hearn would administer a long stick that would inflict pain on guilty children. I entered the classroom in front of the senior third graders and the witchy woman knowing what I was about to face. It was Finkelstein vs. Yanofsky and I waived my right to a lawyer. Tears rolled down my cheek as the ever powerful Miss O'Hearn gave me a frozen stare and then in a calm voice asked, "Do you know what you did?" With my voice cracking from fear, I said, "Yes, I know." My mind raced to the ultimate conclusion. I would be administered the 'rat hand' and humiliated in front of Miss O'Hearn's third grade class. The wicked witch of the west scolded me and warned me not to do that again. I said, "Ok, Miss O'Hearn," and left her classroom. I was certainly relieved. No rat hand for me.

Two years later upon graduation, I wondered if the 'rat hand' really ever existed. I don't know who ever started those rumors in the first place. Maybe it was Joey Finkelstein.

How did Godzilla and King Kong get into this book? That's an easy one. It brings me to the story of the first time I ever gambled. I was a busy guy in the early 60's and on a Saturday afternoon my parents drove me and my buddy to the fancy schmancy Oriental Theater in Mattapan Square. It would be my very first movie. The price of a movie ticket in those care-free times was sixty-nine-cents. With popcorn on my lap, I was well-prepared and extremely excited to watch Godzilla battle King Kong on the biggest screen I had ever seen! The excitement of what was about to happen, along with my heavily buttered popcorn, was not enough. I had to have a bit more action for some reason. I bet my buddy five-cents on the outcome. I took Godzilla, he took King Kong. My reasoning was this. Kong was awfully strong, but the ability to breathe fire absolutely had to give Godzilla the edge. As the two of them trampled their way through New York City, destroying everything in their path, it was obvious that their final duel would take place in the Hudson River. It was at that point that I came to the realization that doing battle under water could neutralize Godzilla's fire-breathing advantage. I was on the edge of my seat as the two mega-monsters went toe-to-toe in the Hudson River. On top of this very dramatic scene, I remembered that I had a nickel on the line. The fight raged on and then suddenly there was a calm that permeated throughout the theater and in this case, the Hudson River. Then, one of the creatures slowly emerged. It was mighty King Kong. Kong was still the king and I lost the bet. Then I thought, where was I going to get the five cents?

Before leaving the 'Dorchest-ah section of my book, I'd be re-miss if I didn't tell you the story of the incredible family that lived on the third floor of our building in the projects; the Frank family. It was 1964. The Frank's left Dorchester and moved to Jamaica Plain, our family headed south to Randolph. A few years later we learned more about the horrible battles that the Frank's fought against Huntington's Disease. I wrote the following excerpt many years later about the tragic fate of my childhood neighbors and the fund-raising event called the Hoop-A-Thon. This appeared in the Huntington's Disease Society Association's New England News edition.

Finding a cure for Huntington's Disease

If I'm so lucky (and I am) then there must be something that has happened in my life that makes me feel this way....something or someone that hasn't been so lucky. Well, here goes the ultimate example. For the past two decades, I've been involved in a charity basketball event that benefits a little-known disease called Huntington's Disease. HD is a degenerative disease that affects the mind and body. The symptoms of HD are described as having ALS, Parkinson's and Alzheimer's-simultaneously. It's a dreadful inherited disease with no known cure. Just about 53 years ago I grew up in Dorchester in the projects, across from Franklin Field. Along with the Bahn family, we all became great friends. When I think about it, since I was just seven years old, these were really the first friends I ever had. The Frank family was made up of Sumner, who was a doctor, his wife, Natalie, and their four children; Jonathan, Jamie, Andy and Claudia. When the Franks moved to Jamaica Plain and we moved to Randolph, we still kept in touch and stayed pretty close.

Years later, we learned that Sumner Frank showed symptoms of HD and eventually it took his life. I learned more and more about Huntington's Disease. First, that my four childhood friends had a 50/50 chance of inheriting HD. Natalie was the brave and proud mother, not quite knowing everything that was about to happen to her family. One by one, Jonathan, Andy, Claudia and Jamie learned that they in fact had the disease.

It was devastating. I couldn't understand how Natalie's lot in life was to watch her four children's physical and mental condition worsen every single day. It was at that time that I participated in HD's annual hoop-a-thon event that took place at Boston College. With Natalie heading the fund-raising table and her children in attendance, hundreds of special people, led by the incredible May Long, took over the Boston College gymnasium, shooting foul shots, raising money hoping that someday a cure will be found.

Jonathan Frank, who at an early age was your basic childhood genius and the oldest of four children, followed his father to an early death in his 40's. One by one, all four children passed on, as Natalie fought her daily battle to save them. How could you not admire the strength of this very special lady? For two decades, I participated in the annual Hoop-a-thon event to honor Natalie and all the incredible families I've met that have contracted the disease. The premise of the event was to step up to the foul line, shoot foul shots for either five or ten minutes with the help of an assembly line of volunteer rebounders. Basically, you'd be handed a basketball every couple of seconds, race against the clock and hopefully sink as many baskets as possible. Each shooter would contact friends and family to sponsor them. Their donation would either be a flat fee or based on the number of baskets that you could sink during the allotted time.

One year, I hit 174 foul shots in 10 minutes. More importantly it meant that I was able to raise more money for the cause. There was a Boston College assistant basketball coach that same day that sank 274 in 10 minutes. He was like a machine out there. Former and current celebrities made a number of appearances to support the event. Former Boston newsman Jim Boyd, weatherman Harvey Leonard, Mark Rosenthal and Dick Albert participated. Local sports hero Doug Flutie, Mayor Flynn and Senator Scott Brown also made appearances at the

Hoop-a-thon. One celebrity, however, stands above the rest and that's Jackie MacMullan, the great Hall of Fame sportswriter and personality from *The Boston Globe, Sports Illustrated* and *ESPN.* Through the years, Jackie has given a tremendous amount of her time to support the event. I learned that Jackie was also a basketball star at the University of New Hampshire in Durham and was quite an athlete. I have to say that one of my favorite memories was playing alongside Jackie Mac at one of the Hoop-a-thon events and recording a higher score. Well, hold on Stevie boy. I learned soon after that prior to the event, she had jammed her hand and was shooting the basketball while hurt. So much for beating my sports writing idol! Not only is Jackie a talented writer, but without a doubt, one of the nicest people on the planet.

Not long after the Hoop-a-thon events, I had the honor of emceeing an HD event called "Talkin' Smack with Jackie Mac." The event was spearheaded by a wonderful lady, Virginia Goolkasian. Prior to the festivities, I wanted to do as much research as possible so that I would be able to serve as an adequate and informed emcee. My research led me to two of her colleagues at *The Boston Globe*; the legendary Bob Ryan and the great Dan Shaughnessy. They gave me some fantastic material for my introduction. Our conversations had one common theme: everyone liked Jackie Mac. Ryan talked about how when Jackie broke into the business he considered her, in baseball terms, a .285 hitter. Not surprised, but recognizing the obvious, he told me that Jackie turned into a .325 hitter in the sports writing industry. Maybe that's why she was the first female writer to be inducted into the Naismith Basketball Hall of Fame.

"Talking Smack with Jackie Mac" was held at the Marriott Courtyard Charles River Ballroom in Cambridge and was a huge success, raising thousands of dollars to help find a cure for Huntington's Disease. To this day, they still haven't found a cure, but the research aggressively continues.

I've decided to donate the proceeds from the sales of this book to the Huntington's Disease Society of America in memory of the Frank family and the hopes that the future of those struck by this crippling disease will see the day when a cure is found.

MEMORABLE HOOP-A-THON PICS

Left to right Lou Yanofsky, Jamie, Natalie and Jonathan Frank, Jacqui and Steve Yanofsky.

Me, Harvey Zack, Mark Weiner, Meredith and Daniel Yanofsky (front)

Jackie MacMullan, Scott Brown and friends.

Audrey Hackett, photo bomber, Charlie and Nathaniel Hackett, Harvey Zack, Me and Jenni Dunn.

Jackie Mac, me, Harvey Zack and Mark Weiner

CHAPTER TWO

Entering Randolph: Taffy Apples, the RBA, the 100-yard Dash and the Invisible Jukebox

In 1964, we moved to Randolph, located about 12 miles south of Boston. It was a scary transition for me at the ripe old age of 11, leaving my best friends and familiar turf. The good news was that we were about to live in our own home at our new address, 16 Clark Street. It was a large, beige duplex with a spacious back yard and a four-car driveway. My Aunt Carole and Uncle Marshall, along with my cousins, Lloyd and Rhonda, lived in the other half of the duplex. I was now a fifth grader at the EG Lyons School, conveniently located at the end of the street. I was a bit shy, just like my initials S.H.Y., but it didn't take me long to get comfortable and meet a slew of new friends. I actually won the title of class president in my first year without campaigning for a single day!

It was at that time that I grew curious about the opposite sex. As class president I had some clout and chose Gloria as my first girlfriend. I quickly discovered that the key to our successful relationship was that we never spoke a word to each other. I'm not sure that she even knew that she was my girlfriend. Still, we had this magical special bond. Gloria would bring her friends and sit on the foundation of a new, yet to be built home, directly across the street from where I lived. Me and my buddy Doug, with guitars in hand, would sing from my room on the second floor while blasting music from Manfred Mann, Dave Clark Five and the Beatles. The girls would dance on a wooden platform, making us feel like rock stars. One day while performing, it started to rain. My mother wanted to invite the girls into the house. "No, don't do that" I yelled at the top of my lungs. God forbid I'd actually have to talk to my girlfriend. Yes, I was still a bit shy and actually didn't even know how to play the guitar at that point. Gloria was in my class and sat right across the aisle. We exchanged notes occasionally, but still never spoke a word. Love is strange, don't you think?

In Randolph it was raining friends. Mike Locke, Roger, Billy and Kenny Elliott; Marc Golding, Mark and Jeff Weiner, Al Goldberg, Barry Stone, Doug Marram, Rich Stone and Jay Hecht, just to name a few. My love of sports took over my young life. We added a basketball hoop in front of our home attached to a telephone pole. Shortly after that I established a new basketball league for me and my buddies. It was called the R.B.A., which was short for Randolph Basketball Association. The games would consist of two-on-two match-ups and believe it or not, we kept all of the statistics. I have them to this day in a manila folder. Roger Elliott, known as the Big E was the tallest of the group. There were days when Roger and I would play one on one games up to 100. These days it's difficult to play a one-on-one game up to five. Roger was a good six inches taller than I. In my efforts to get the ball over his out-stretched hands, the famous lefty hook was born. We had some classic match-ups, resting occasionally to let cars pass by. There would be cold, snowy wintry days that we would actually shovel the street to get the games in. Let the record show that Roger was the all-time leading scorer and I was in second place. The big E registered 434 points, and I scored 369. Mike Locke scored 232 and Rich Stone was the last of the 200-point scorers with 201. The season lasted 20 games before it disbanded.

Even in those days it was clear to me that I wanted to pursue a career as a sportscaster. I would play wiffle ball in my driveway and then engage in a fictitious game against some stiff competition….myself. I would then copy the batting stances of some of my favorite ballplayers, like Yaz, Willie Mays, Willie McCovey, and then proceed to toss the ball up in the air and hit it. Simultaneously I would announce the game out loud. I don't think that the neighbors ever approached my parents to ask them if everything was all right with their son.

Our home at 16 Clark Street was pretty much the gathering spot for my friends. As I mentioned, we shared our duplex home with my aunt and uncle and my cousins Rhonda and Lloyd. My Uncle Marshall was a musician. He had a tremendous voice and sang in a band. He had changed his name from Yanofsky to Young and thus the band's name was the Marshall Young Orchestra. Rumor has it that he changed his name so that it could fit on the front of the drum set. I guess they didn't make a drum large enough to fit the name Yanofsky. He played the bass, a huge bulky instrument that was pretty much kept in our hallway in between his gigs. Marshall was my father's younger brother and Al was his older brother. Al was known as Uncle Bing because he sounded like Bing

Crosby. Uncle Bing's specialty was singing "Pennies from Heaven," and at family celebrations it was a tradition that while he was crooning away, all of us would throw pennies directly at him.

My Uncle Marshall and my Dad had become partners in a candy store called Adam's Apple. Isn't it the dream of most young people to have their family own a candy store? The store was located about a half hour away in the Taunton Mall.

My father made taffy apples and fudge and hired many of my friends in the process. They were the best taffy apples; not the kind that got stuck in your teeth, and his fudge was out of this world. My brother and I, along with my mother and several friends, would work to make the taffy apples in a small store in Dorchester. It was amazing to see the process that was involved. A couple of us would be in charge of skewering the apples or another way to put it, shoving the sticks into the fresh MacIntosh apples before they would be put in a scalding pot of sugar and coloring that would be used to coat the apples. The role of the "dipper" was critical. That person would dip the apples into the pot, giving them a proper spin before placing them in the coconut. The "coconut-er" would cover the apple with the coconut and place them on an adjacent tray. When the apples cooled down, someone (usually my father) would pack the finished product. Other than the candy store sales, my dad also sold them at wholesale to neighborhood convenient stores. In addition we would peddle our taffy apples every year at the famous St. Patrick's Day parade in South Boston. My father would hire me and my brother Ken and friends to walk the streets of Southie selling our delicious product. I remember working the parades and taking the orders from Dad. He never let up on any of us and really taught me a great lesson on how to hustle. Even more so, he taught me the importance of a strong work ethic. I carried that with me throughout my work life for sure.

Back to the neighborhood...

Growing up in Randolph, there were several brother combinations in our neighborhood, but no one had as good a relationship as me and my brother Kenny In fact, most of the brother combinations didn't get along. Even though there was a four year age difference between Kenny and I, my friends became his friends and vice versa. Those were certainly the good old days. No computers, cell phones or video games.

Life was all about when the next game would take place. Would it be street football, more basketball, baseball or hockey? Life was care-free and we were having the time of our lives, even though we didn't realize it then.

Fast forward to Randolph High School. Most of my memories were tied to my sports activities. I was a decent athlete, albeit very skinny. My mother would always joke that she could count my ribs even though she fed me quite well. I played varsity track and basketball until my graduation in 1971. To this day I tell people that I ran the 100-yard dash in 10.5 seconds and that was just one second off the world record. Now that's a fact. However, if you know anything about track, then you know that one second off a world record is like an eternity in a short sprint like the 100-yard dash. It sounded good though, didn't it? Hey, that still meant that I could really fly on the track.

In my junior year I was named to represent Randolph High School at the New England finals to be staged at White Stadium in Dorchester. My events that day would include the 100-yard dash (my specialty) and the relay race. Out of the four runners representing Randolph High School, I would run the third leg of the relay. Each sprinter would run 220 yards. Our team got off to a rocky start and trailed the field in a big way. As I tried to make up ground and approached the anchor, Ira Korch, he waved to me as if to say, "forget about it, we're so far behind, so take it easy." The 100-yard dash wasn't any better. I was excited nonetheless to get the chance to represent my high school featuring the top eight sprinters in the state. Not to mention that there were 2,000 people in the stands watching the action and cheering for their favorite school. Next came the introduction of the runners. I had never ever heard my name announced over a PA system before. The tension and stress continued to build prior to race time. I looked around to catch a glimpse at the competition and a wave of insecurity swept all over my skinny body. I asked myself, what the heck am I doing here? I glanced again at some of the top sprinters in the state. All of the race participants were at least 6-feet 3-inches tall and six of those feet were nothing but legs. And then there was me, 5-feet 7-inches, scrawny and overmatched before the race even started. It was the power of negative thinking or to put it another away, I had psyched myself out. Keep in mind that my best time in the 100-yard dash was a respectable 10.5 seconds, and my average time was 10.7 seconds. I set myself in the running blocks, looked ahead concentrating on the sound of the starting gun. For some reason, I glanced yet again at some of the competitors. In that split second my focus had evaporated. The gun went off and I left the blocks trailing the field. Well, 10.4 seconds later, the race was over and my finish was predictable that day. I ran the 100 hundred-yard dash in 11.2 seconds, my worst time of the year. The track coach, Mal Hill, greeted me at the finish line, surprised and disappointed at the outcome. He looked at me astonishingly and said, "What happened?" I responded with the most direct answer that I could come up with. "Hey coach, did you ever have a bad day?"

During my senior year at Randolph High School, Roger Elliott, Barry Stone and myself headed north on Route 93 to visit our friend Mike Locke at Tufts University. The game plan was to eat dinner, sleep over, and whatever else that might happen at a college campus. Mike and Roger were one year ahead of me and we were all very close. The weather that day was atrocious. It was blizzard like conditions (which I always referred to as Fresca, based on the TV commercial). We arrived at Mike's dorm room and were quickly introduced to his roommate, Hans. The room was dark and we could hardly see Mike's roomie. The ceiling was covered with black wallpaper with tiny holes that were made to look like stars. Hans was sitting on the floor, legs crossed. Directly in front of him was a large orange ball on a string suspended from the ceiling (you can't make this stuff up). Hans was a bit distracted as the orange ball rotated in a not so perfect circle. Hans with his eyes fixated and focused on the ball, kept repeating, "What a mindbender!" My first thought was, "Steve, you're not in Randolph anymore." I felt way out of my element, but wanted to fit in during my very first college experience. I believe that the drug being circulated in the room was hashish. This was new to me and yet after about an hour of watching the orange ball and puffs on the bong, I felt fine, unaffected by the drug, while the others were giggling and not very coherent. "What a mindbender," I kept hearing over and over again. At that point we took a peek outside of the dorm's snow covered window. Yes, we were in the middle of a doozy of a blizzard. Somehow we heard that there were lots of cars stuck in the snow and that people needed help. So we got off the floor and left the smoke-filled room, heading out to do our good deed for the evening. For some reason, we all headed out without wearing our jackets. I guess it didn't matter that it was 10 degrees outside. We moved a few cars out of at least a foot of snow and then returned to the dorm, soaking wet and freezing, but glad that we helped.

We warmed up a bit and all of us came to the conclusion that we were absolutely starving. Hans suggested that we head down the hill to Dunkin' Donuts. That sounded like a great game plan to me. If memory serves me correctly, I think that I ate at least six donuts. Never ate that many donuts in one sitting. Then, I proceeded to the jukebox, put in 50-cents and played mind-bending tunes by the Doors and the Beatles. I was really digging the college scene and felt pretty cool. We returned to the dorm and slept for two hours or so. The next morning we headed back to Dunkin' Donuts for breakfast. When we walked in to order I noticed that the juke box was missing. I asked the manager what had happened to the juke box. He said to me, "This is Dunkin' Donuts, we've never had a juke box." OK then, I guess that I'll have to admit that hallucinating a jukebox, moving cars out of a foot of snow without a jacket, and eating six donuts was most likely the workings of this drug called hash. A wave of guilt came over me, not because of the drugs. I could only think about last night and wondered what my mother would've said if she knew that I went outside in a blizzard without wearing a jacket!

CHAPTER THREE

College Days: The Draft, Fenway's Bleachers and an Attempt at Love

The next trip on my life's journey was attending college. It was getting close to the time when I really needed to grow up and figure out what I was going to do with my life. I had applied to Curry College in Milton, Emerson College and Boston University. I wanted to attend a school that might further my broadcasting and writing skills. I chose Boston University and the College of Basic Studies. As a commuter, I didn't really have the opportunity to experience the college life. My challenge was to avoid getting a ticket on Commonwealth Ave and beat the Storrow Drive rush hour traffic home. Some of my commuting time was spent on the Jamaicaway. Did anyone ever drive on that horrendous stretch of roadway? Two narrow lanes that could barely fit two people riding their bicycles side by side. The Jamaicaway was not my best option home but at times was necessary. In fact, a few years before college, I went on my road test for my driver's license. Maybe the driver education instructor wasn't too fond of me because he took me to, of all places, the Jamaicaway! A true test of mental strength! Somehow I passed the test.

Back to my biggest daily challenge. Public enemy number one: meter maids. They were vicious and ruthless. On one side of Commonwealth Ave, you couldn't park there prior to 9:30 am. The other side, you couldn't park after 4:00 pm. That set up an interesting challenge for me as a commuter, attempting to attend my classes without accumulating parking tickets. When I had a 9:30 class, I would sit in my car until it was time to go. But, because you couldn't park there until 9:30 am, the gestapo would come over to me and rudely say, "You can't park here." I told her that I understood, but then would sit in my car hoping she'd continue down Commonwealth Ave to find and ticket the car of her next victim. A few minutes passed, and I see the same meter maid running towards me, her arms flailing about, and her face turning red as she approached my vehicle. She was gasping for air trying to catch her breath and proceeded to order me to leave. Of course my next class was just five minutes away from starting. The meter maid stared at me until I left this perfect parking spot. So, I proceeded to drive around to find another space. Did you ever drive around Boston and come to the inevitable conclusion that there are no parking spaces left in the entire city? Well, I found a space and proceeded to sprint to my class. I was 10 minutes late. Following the class, I once again had to feed the meter. Since I parked a good distance away, I knew I was cutting it very close and there was a chance that the meter would expire. Lo and behold, there she was, the same meter maid that I encountered an hour before. I was about twenty yards away and I saw a parking ticket on my windshield. Ugghh! I guess timing is everything, right? I couldn't win no matter where I parked. Lovely Rita, meter maid (a popular Beatles tune) she was not! I had received 25 tickets during my first three years at B.U. until one day a friend from Randolph gave me some valuable advice. Normie graduated high school with me and was also a commuting student. Remember that the meters in those days included a crank. You'd put in your dime and crank it till it accepted your payment. My buddy unveiled a plan for me that worked very well for him. First, he suggested that I spray paint the meter black and the mean meter maid would walk on by. I didn't like that. The second idea I found interesting. Put your dime into the slot, then turn the crank and tie a rubber band into the groove of the crank. That will jam the meter and the time left will not move. Still a devious way to solidify a parking spot, but in frustration I gave it a shot.

Throughout my senior year, I received exactly one parking ticket.

My college experience wasn't the greatest as a commuter. No real social life to speak of, but I did what I had to do to get to graduation. During my four years at B.U., I formed friendships with Mike Remarski from Rhode Island, Tony Lando from Waltham and Julian Williams from Savannah, Georgia.

One memory that stands out during my time at Boston University was the day of the military draft. I sat in class with my buddies waiting to see if our college life would be interrupted and that some of us may be on our way to Vietnam. Going back to 1968, President Richard M. Nixon had promised to end the draft. There was much debate on the draft issue and decisions were weighed over the next few years. One of the questions was could we survive with an all-volunteer army and lower the temperature of those young adults who were protesting the Vietnam War. On February 2, 1972, a draft lottery was held to determine priority numbers for men born in 1953, the year I was born. I was scared to death and so were my B.U. buddies. My parents did not want me to go to Vietnam and told me if I'm drafted, we'd move to Canada. I brought my transistor radio to the lecture hall that day with earplugs. In front of me I had concocted a new kind of scorecard. It was a list of my friends who were born in 1953 and their birthdates. It felt like a game of Russian Roulette, but this time with our futures in jeopardy and to be decided by a random drawing. If your birthdate was drawn with numbers 1 through 50, you would be drafted. The moments that followed brought relief to some and anger and fear to others. As the numbers were drawn I would write a note to my buddies when I heard their birth dates called. "Hey Tony, you got 252, Mike, you got 275, nice going!" As the day went on, there was only one birth date that I might've missed when it was called. That one was mine, May 30, 1953. The radio broadcast was complete and I still didn't know what fate had in store for me. I called my mother on the phone and asked if she was aware as to what had happened. She sounded a bit melancholy and she spoke very softly. "Oh, you didn't hear, you got number 48." My heart sank. She repeated to me that we'd all be moving to Canada. I sat in that study hall a bit longer than needed. It was no longer filled with my fellow classmates. I would most likely be one of the last ones to go to war because of the draft lottery system.

Not too long after that, it was announced by Secretary of Defense Melvin Laird that the draft lottery that day would be null and void. Whew! I could breathe again. It would then be announced that during the month of March and the years of 1973, 1974 and 1975, the Selective Service would assign draft priority numbers for all men born in 1954, 1955 and 1956, in case the draft was extended, but it never was. For me and my family, we would stay put on the South Shore in the quaint town of Randolph. Canada would have to do without the Yanofsky family. That was quite a relief to say the least.

My college life as a commuter consisted of driving fifteen miles to BU, avoiding the meter maids on Commonwealth Avenue, beating the Storrow Drive traffic home, studying and then back to classes the next day. Some days I carpooled with fellow Randolphian Franceen Raffelson, who lived on Green Street, one street over from me. There was very little college life. No college parties either. That was the plight of the commuter. Now, I don't want you to think that college was all bad. My friends Tony, Mike and I would meet prior to our American Film class, a three-hour bore-fest three days a week from 2:00pm-5:00pm. It was a meeting of the minds when major decisions were made. We would weigh our options. The choices were American Film or skipping out to see the Boston Red Sox at Fenway for a matinee game. On any nice day when the sun was shining, the decision was easy. We paid 50-cents and enjoyed the Sox games from Fenway's bleacher seats. Don't tell my mother that one.

During my time at B.U., I worked at WTBU, the student-run radio station doing what else, sportscasting. The legendary Howard Stern actually graced the airwaves at Boston University, graduating one year after I did. There was one girl at B.U. who also grew up in my hometown of Randolph. Her name was Paula Ernest. We knew each other from the old hood but didn't really have any kind of close friendship. I simply admired her from afar. In addition, she had a boyfriend, but I was hoping that someday that boyfriend would be me. Definitely a long shot or maybe just a fantasy, but I thought I'd give it a try. I would leave notes in her dorm mailbox. The note would explain that I would be on the air at 5:15pm the next day and that I would appreciate if she could listen and then give me her opinion of the report. Yes, I know. It was a very feeble attempt at love. I doubt if she ever listened. After a year of pursuing Paula, I had almost given up when I got a phone call from my good friend Nancy Barroll. She told me that Paula and her boyfriend had broken up. Nancy suggested that now was a good time for me to make my move. I tried to use my Yanofsky charm on her and at first was a bit too pushy and I almost blew it. I had a personal dating discussion with myself, configured a new dating strategy, and it finally worked! If you haven't guessed it by now, that girl Paula would become my bride seven years later.

I graduated Boston University in 1975 with a Bachelor of Science Degree in Public Communications. The following year I would attend Northeast Broadcasting School. It was a one-year course that gave more practical training. In fact, I often kidded that I learned more in one year at Northeast Broadcasting School than I did at four years at B.U. Victor Best was the owner of the school, located at the corner of Fairfield and Marlborough Streets in Boston's Back Bay. Vin Rafferty was my favorite instructor. He was instrumental in providing me with the knowledge that was necessary to pursue a career in radio, including a class on how to conduct yourself in an interview setting. I really enjoyed my time at Northeast Broadcasting School. In fact, they were the reason that I landed my first radio job in Portsmouth in 1977

Unfortunately, in June of 1977 our family was thrown a devastating curveball. My friends and I were playing baseball on the street outside our home at 16 Clark Street when a police car drove up with my Aunt Carole and cousin Rhonda. I was thinking that they had gotten a flat tire somewhere. As the police officer got out of his vehicle, I kidded with him saying, "What did they do now?" He wasn't laughing. He told me that my aunt and cousins Lloyd and Rhonda had stopped for gas at a station in Braintree. The gas station was very busy that day and Lloyd had gotten out of the car to pump the gas for his mother. Just as he was tightening the gas cap, a 77-year old man backed into Lloyd pinning him between the two cars. The policeman told me that despite efforts to save him, Lloyd didn't make it. We called Dad who was working at his candy store and told him to come home right away, that there had been a terrible accident. When he arrived, he was walking towards the front of the house when he found out the news. I remember him falling to the ground in horror and disbelief. Lloyd was only fifteen years old. We were completely devastated What could we possibly say to Aunt Carole and Uncle Marshall? There was nothing to say. Incredible sorrow cut us all so deeply. Lloyd was just starting out in life as a young energetic man and then in a quick second, his life was taken away. Lloyd was such a great kid and everything that a fifteen year-old should be. That moment would change our lives forever. We think of Lloyd often and will never forget his handsome, smiling face. To this day, I have wonderful conversations with my Aunt Carole. She's an amazing woman and I have so much respect for her. Her love of people knows no bounds and her positive nature is infectious to everyone she meets. I love my Aunt Carole so much. Wish all of you could meet her.

41 Years in Radio

(1977-2018)

WBBX, Portsmouth, NH   1977-1980

WKBR/Manchester, NH   1981-1985

WCGY/WCCM/Lawrence, Ma   1986-1994

WSSH/Oasis Boston, Ma   1995-1996

WROR/Boston, Ma   1997-2004

WXRV/Haverhill, Ma   2004-2017

Valley 98.9/Methuen, Ma   2018-2018

CHAPTER FOUR

Radio: In the Beginning

1977 was my first year in radio. It was the year of *Star Wars*, disco dancing and the TV mini-series, *Roots*. Jimmy Carter became our 39th president and *Annie Hall* won the Oscar for Best Film. (my all-time favorite movie).

After graduating from Boston University and Victor Best's Northeast Broadcasting School, it was time to get a real job, hopefully in the world of sports. Of all the places in New England, somehow my first radio interview was out in the boondocks of Maine, specifically Millinocket, Maine. No wonder after six hours of driving in my big green gas-guzzling 1968 Pontiac Catalina, I arrived looking less than fresh to say the least. As I approached the radio station's address, I was a bit surprised to see that it was nothing more than an old white oversized trailer. As I entered, I was greeted by two Siamese cats and an older couple that I presumed were the owners. The husband and wife combination were extremely laid back and cordial to me. I was very excited because I knew that regardless where the radio station was, this could be my big break! After a brief discussion, Mr. And Mrs. Millinocket described the job's duties. Turn on the transmitter in the morning, read the news, weather and sports, then play music ranging from Sinatra to the Beatles. At the conclusion of the day I'd be sweeping the floors and then taking out the garbage. I was confident that I could do all those things. The job was to pay $100 a week. My mind was racing. I was going to get $100 a week to just write and read sports, and yes the other stuff as well. Sounds like a good deal to me!

Now it was time for my first on-air audition. As I began to read, the cats immediately took a liking to my right leg. Could that have been part of the owners' strategy, to see if I could overcome distractions and still come through with a flawless Paul Harvey like read? Well, I came through with flying colors and at the same time fell in love with the two cats. The owners praised my off the cuff performance. I knew then that they were going to offer me the job. Maybe it was because I was the only one that showed up to be interviewed. At this point, I thought

I'd ask some questions. Being the type that likes to go out to some good restaurants, perhaps take in a movie or attend a sporting event, I asked, "What's Millinocket like?" Enthusiastically they answered, "If you love hunting and fishing, this is the place to be. Movies? You'd have to drive to Bangor, about 65 miles or so down the road." At that point, they left the room, giving me the chance to have my own private meeting with myself. My first thought was that I really needed a shower. My second thought was 'oy vey.' My third thought was that I was actually going to be *on the air!* It was a dream come true! Didn't even matter that the overall listening audience was made up of only about 100 people and could only be heard within a three to five-mile radius from the broadcast trailer.

Eventually, most of my Millinocket groupies would have children which meant to me, more listeners. Actually, upon further review, Millinocket's population in 1977 was 7,500, so Steve Yanofsky would actually be announcing to thousands of listeners. An audience that would be listening to my every word, depending on me for their daily dose of news, sports and weather. So the numbers didn't really matter. What did matter was that I was going to be a one-man show with my own stage to show the world how great an announcer I really am. I'm so humble, don't you think?

Well, through my training and some common sense, it was important for me to show my prospective bosses an air of confidence, yet at the same time not appear too cocky. Whatever I said and how I said it seemed to have worked. They quickly offered me the $100 a week pay day and I told them that I would be back in touch when I returned home. I hugged the two of them and thanked them. The two Siamese cats showed a bit of jealousy by hissing at me as I walked out the door of the trailer.

On the way home, I found a phone booth at a Millinocket gas station and phoned my parents to tell them about the interview and the job offer. I barely got the news out of my mouth when my mother told me that I got a phone call from WBBX radio in Portsmouth, New Hampshire. I had sent my resume to them a few months back and never heard from them, until now. They wanted to talk to me about a sports position during their three-hour news block. Boy, when it rains, it pours!

All of a sudden, one year out of college and broadcasting school, my services were in demand. Didn't matter that being a

New Englander, I still couldn't pronounce my "r"s correctly (Pahk the cah in hahvid yahd). In my attempt to properly announce that tricky letter, I found myself adding "r"s to words that didn't have any. For instance, "How would you like to go out for a pizz-er?" (pizza)

So now, it looks like I may very well have two jobs to consider; the life of hunting and fishing and working alongside two adorable Siamese cats in Millinocket, Maine, or a sports job at WBBX in Portsmouth, New Hampshire, known as the "Power of the Seacoast!"

Now, I'm sure that if you're reading this book, that most of you know me fairly well. And you're familiar with the fact that I eat, drink and sleep sports. Always have, always will. The chance to be 'on-the-air' doing play-by-play basketball and football and a sports talk show, well, for me it was the cat's meow, so to speak. That would be nirvana! Plus, Portsmouth, New Hampshire was a pretty cool place in 1977 (and still is) and I would be living closer to home, only an hour away. No offense to the fine people of Millinocket, Maine, but the decision was obvious. So, even though it was a part-time job, just 15 hours a week, I took the ball, not the shotgun and ran with it. I called Millinocket and politely turned down their generous $100 a week offer, effectively putting an end to my Jack London experience.

WBBX, the "Power of the Seacoast," would be my first job in radio and my first time away from home. I would now live at the Meadowbrook Motor Inn adjacent to the Portsmouth rotary and pay $40 per week for rent. No kitchen, no anything, just a bed, four walls, a yellow lamp and a tiny bathroom. But, who cared? I was now a radio star! Nothing or no one could stop me now. I remember my first day on the job with WBBX's program director, Jim Metcalf. The first thing he asked me was what would be my on-air name? I never really thought of that. My name was Steve Yanofsky I was proud of that name and assumed that's what I would use on the air. Jim said, "How about Steve Young?" He was almost telling me that would be my name rather than asking. So, who was I to argue? From that day moving forward, my radio name would be Steve Young.

Jim Metcalf had a habit of wearing sunglasses, even when he was inside the radio station. Since this was my first job in radio, I figured that maybe all program directors were hip and wearing sunglasses made them even more hip. Jim Metcalf might have been a bit ahead of his time. When I think back, he reminded me of Dr. Johnny Fever, disc jockey from the popular TV sitcom *WKRP in Cincinnati*. Fever, who was played by actor Howard Hesseman, often wore sunglasses for whatever reason. However after further review, I learned that *WKRP in Cincinnati* didn't air till 1978. So, the indoor sunglasses thing was simply the hip style of James Metcalf.

At that point, he asked me to read for him as a mini audition. After a few minutes, he said to me. "When you go on the air, you have to make believe that you're talking to your friends and that will relax you." He proceeded to draw a smiley face on the microphone and asked me to read again. I thought that was pretty sound advice. I was open to anything at that point during my quest to someday be a famous sportscaster.

To supplement my miniscule sports job income, I landed a position as a men's sportswear salesman at Kimball's in the Newington Mall. My typical day looked like this. .Get up at 4:30am, be at the radio station by 5:15 am, prepare my sports reports and then be on the air every half hour from 6:00am-9:00am. At the conclusion of my radio day, I would then return to the Meadowbrook Motor Inn, change my clothes, head to the mall and make an attempt to sell suits and accessories from 9:30am to 9:30pm. Long day for sure, and all for $2.25 per hour. Didn't matter to me; I was on my own for the very first time and was loving the entire experience. Officially, WBBX was my first radio "family." Little did I know at the time that the WBBX family would be followed by six more radio families. Our hard-hitting news team was led by news director Gene Fisk and reporter Dan Cole. The personable and effervescent Evie Sacks contributed special life-style reports and was quite good. I worked very closely with my new best friend, Sam Bruno. He was the station's sports director, main play-by-play man and was extremely popular amongst the local Portsmouth social scene. Sam knew his sports and it was a great honor for me to learn from him. Sam and I teamed up to do a sports talk show, another dream of mine coming true. I can't believe that I was actually getting paid for talking about sports with local listeners. I don't recall the name of the show, but I know that it lasted for three years.

On the sales side, the likeable Stu Bradley served as the sales manager and Bill Kressman and his family owned the radio station. They had purchased the station from legendary sportscaster Curt Gowdy, who I would later work for at

WCCM/WCGY in Lawrence. After a short stint in my part-time role as a sportscaster, management seemed to like me and was hoping to find a way to give me the opportunity to be at the radio station full-time. After a few meetings, they outlined what my new role would be. I would become the station's bookkeeper/office manager and continue my duties as a sportscaster in the early morning hours. My new role would include payroll, paying the bills, and keeping track of all the numbers, then reporting to management on a daily basis. I certainly thought that the idea of not having to work a second job was a very attractive proposition. When it came to being the office manager, I would receive lots of training from Curt Gowdy's personal bookkeeper, the incredible Gene Silver. Gene was a class-act. A very nice lady who I would have the privilege of working again with in the future. Gene taught me everything she knew and I proceeded to give my unique and new job responsibilities a good shot. I wonder if anyone else out there in radio land had ever worked as a sportscaster/bookkeeper. Well, unfortunately or maybe fortunately, my career as a bookkeeper was short-lived. As much as it was cool to know what everyone was making, it wasn't working. Some people to this day believe that I'm like

Dustin Hoffman's Rain Man when it comes to numbers. In this case, there were simply too many numbers and my heart just wasn't into it. At that point, Stu Bradley, the sales manager, knowing that I loved the idea of being at the radio station full-time, offered me a position on their sales team. Thinking back to my days at Northeast Broadcasting School, the only class that I detested was radio sales. Regardless, I reluctantly accepted the offer, realizing that my sportscasting gig was still part of the deal. I started my sales career off with a big bang. My first sales call resulted in a huge sale (at the time) of $500 to Green's Appliance. It was the easiest $75 bucks I ever made. (15% in commissions) I thought to myself, this sales thing is a piece of cake. Bring on the next victim! Of course, reality set in and my next sale wouldn't show its head for another four weeks.

Being away from home was certainly a tough transition. I was always a home body. Yet my family would visit me on a fairly regular basis and were excited to hear their son on the air. I was a legitimate celebrity in the minds of my mother and father. Always supportive, my beautiful girlfriend Paula would visit me every couple of weeks. Between working long hours, attempting to sell radio advertising, broadcasting sports and getting about five hours a night of sleep, there wasn't much time to do anything else. At 24 years old, I wasn't complaining to anyone, but in the back of mind I would've preferred a full-time position in sports. That was the recurring voice that spoke to me every single night. I would battle that conflicting voice but resigned myself to the fact that I had no time for negative thoughts, just do my job, make my boss happy, sell a ton in the streets of Portsmouth and just maybe someday I'll catch that lucky break as a famous, well-paid sportscaster.

One moment that I didn't enjoy took place at the Meadowbrook Motor Inn on a Sunday morning. Sunday was the only day of the week that I didn't have to get out of bed at 5:00am. At around 6:00am, I heard a big bang outside my apartment window, immediately followed by a phone call from the front desk. The innkeeper shouted in a panicked voice, "Don't move." Half asleep I responded, "How come?" Seemed like a logical response at the time. She told me that a truck hit the columns leading up to my second floor apartment and that the building had become very shaky and might possibly collapse. She then suggested that I walk very gingerly to the stairwell as soon as possible and exit the building. I guess they just didn't make motor inns like they used to. I'm joking, but at the time I was scared to death. I grabbed a bathrobe and headed downstairs to the street level. There were fire trucks and police cars surrounding the area. For some reason it seemed that I was the only rent-paying guest that was asked to evacuate. Luckily, the building didn't collapse. Since I was up anyways on a Sunday morning, I thought that I deserved a great breakfast, so I headed to the Dinnerhorn less than a mile down the street and treated myself to one of my guilty pleasures, pancakes, eggs over easy, orange juice, home fries and bacon, well done please.

I certainly got my feet wet at WBBX. It was a small market radio station but gave me big market opportunities. My first major interview session was with Celtics legend Tommy Heinsohn. With my trusty cassette recorder by my side, I began the interview nervous as all heck. Heinsohn was patient, knowledgeable and offered much insight into the National Basketball Association and my favorite team, the Boston Celtics. Surprisingly, Heinsohn gave me a full three hours. Later on, I would edit the interview into 20 eight-minute segments and use it as a feature over the course of four weeks during my morning sports reports. I have the interview on a reel-to-reel tape somewhere in my basement. I really must find this valuable piece of 'Heinie' memorabilia. By the way, not only was Heinsohn an incredible basketball player and coach, but he was an accomplished artist. Looking back now, how lucky was I to interview a future Hall of Famer in my very first sports interview.

Interview #2 took place a few months later. The Chief, Johnny Bucyk of the Boston Bruins, made the trek to Portsmouth on a Sunday night to be my co-host on a special edition of my sports talk show. I couldn't believe that he was so generous with his time or maybe he heard that I was a hot shot, up and coming sports announcer who had just finished an interview with Tommy Heinsohn. Around my social circles, I was now considered to be the "Larry King of sports talk." Or was that only in my own mind and imagination? Regardless, Johnny Bucyk was one of the nicest sports celebrities that I had ever met. As a Bruin, he devoted hundreds of hours working with children's charities.

The phone lines were jammed as Bucyk answered questions from the WBBX listeners. Tens of thousands of seacoast sports fans tuned in that evening. Ok, maybe it was really hundreds of listeners. Following the show, I asked if he would like to get something to eat at a local bar. Bucyk declined my offer, but instead invited me down to his van. Well, I thought that was strange but I followed the chief down the driveway to where his van was parked. He then proceeded to open the hatch to his trunk. Lo and behold, Bucyk's vehicle was stocked with a full fledged bar! We drank till 2:30 in the morning.

Now as a side note, I should say that hockey was not my forte, but somehow I managed to keep the conversation alive for three more hours. After spending all of that time with Bucyk, I came away with a new and greater appreciation for the sport of hockey. Throughout my sportscasting days, I came to the obvious conclusion that hockey players were much nicer and much more down to earth than any of the other major sports teams. After three years at WBBX, I had gained a wealth of experience, but now it was time for me to move up to the big time, a larger market in the wacky world of radio.

CHAPTER FIVE

Moving on Up to the Queen City

That market was Manchester, New Hampshire. In the early 80's, Portsmouth's population was 26,000, while Manchester boasted 90,000; more than three times the amount of potential sports fans. My audience could triple!

I received a phone call from Al Blake Sr., WKBR's General Manager, to discuss a new opportunity. I was a bit disappointed when I found out that the job offer was primarily in sales with a small possibility that I could still do some sportscasting. My heart told me to go for it. After all, I did have some early success in sales and this was an opportunity for me to make more money. Being a people person, whatever that means, I slowly and reluctantly began to grow more of an interest in the sales process. So, now it was onto my second radio family as well as my second job as an account executive. It's funny, but when I would tell anyone that I sold radio, they assumed that I sold "radios" for a living, i.e. transistor radios, boom boxes, radios with cassette players, etc.

WKBR was located off exit five, route three on the Daniel Webster Highway, next door to Jacques Florists. Its format was adult contemporary music that included an all-star on-air cast. In the AM, Bill Morrissey offered listeners his personable style and possessed a golden voice, perfect for radio. Eddie B. Baker, the opposite of Morrissey in just about every way brought his extraordinary talents to the station. Eddie B. was also an accomplished piano player and entertainer. These were the two main personalities that I would boast about on the streets of Manchester. The sales job at the time was not complicated. It was all about walking into local businesses, finding the owner or advertising decision maker, and then putting together a marketing plan that they could afford. No client needs analysis questions in 1981, just develop and nurture strong relationships, write a radio commercial (called a spec spot) and close the deal.

Al Blake, Jr. was the Sales Manager. Al knew everyone and was a hustler on the streets but in a very good way. These were the days I was developing my own sales technique and I certainly learned a lot from Al. It was all about customer service, genuinely caring for your clients, and doing everything you could to make them succeed. I followed that philosophy for the next three decades and five more radio stations that would follow. When I arrived at WKBR, it wasn't exactly a ratings winner. WZID-95.7 was the top dog. I couldn't rely on ratings and I believe that I became a better salesman because of it. While WZID sales guys and gals were spouting their ratings and asked clients to sign on the dotted line, I would develop relationships with area businesses, small, medium and large. Then I would take pride in writing and producing customized radio commercials for their company. The entire process took longer, but the end result most of the time resulted in a sale, and then I would work hard to make the campaign work.

I always wondered if salespeople working at radio stations with strong ratings could switch to a station with no numbers and still be successful. The ratings or lack thereof would be a common theme throughout my 41 years in the broadcast industry. The battle cry in those days was "live by the numbers, die by the numbers." Of course, it would've been nice to have the ratings to boast about, but after years of reflection, I liked the way it came out.

The station also had a softball team as well as a very cool mascot, Mr. Moose. Al Blake, Jr. normally put the costume on to entertain the children. I volunteered once or twice and it was 175-degrees in that thing! Al was a good sport and would do anything to make the radio station successful.

At WKBR, we covered a number of local college and high school sports. This is where I met the talented Dick Lutsk. I would do just about anything to have a voice like his. His golden tones and his professional delivery of the action was major market material. In my mind, he was as good as anyone I ever heard do play-by-play basketball. I served as his color analyst until he left the radio station. That gave me the opportunity to take over as the play-by-play announcer for the New Hampshire College Penman as well as the St. Anselm Hawks, both located in Manchester. We played teams such as Stonehill College, Assumption College, Bryant University and travelled to Connecticut to battle Sacred Heart University and the University of Bridgeport. There were times when for some reason we took on Division 1 schools like Boston College and Harvard University. Major mismatches but it was still cool to say, "Hello, this is Steve Young from the Conte Forum at Boston College. Tonight, St. Anselm will battle the BC Eagles."

Lots happened during my four years in Manchester, including an ownership change, a switch in the format and a massive turnover in on-air jocks and salespeople. That's when Janice Bailey and Charlie Dent entered my life; Charlie as the General Manager and Janice as the Program Director. We really clicked as a team. Soon after they arrived at the station, the music format changed to "nostalgia." Frank Sinatra, Count Basie, Ella Fitzgerald, Glenn Miller, Sarah Vaughn, Tony Bennett and Louis Armstrong dominated the playlist. The "nostalgia" format certainly gave us our very own niche in the marketplace.

Charlie, Janice and myself worked closely together to develop the format based on the music we all loved. I even suggested an idea that we purchase a restaurant and call it, "WKBR, the Restaurant." I envisioned a 'nostalgia' menu that would include Steak Sinatra, filet of Fitzgerald and Basie burgers. Charlie and Janice loved the idea but of course it was only a pipedream of mine and we stuck with what we knew best.

At WKBR, I got the chance to meet Janice's incredible husband Ken, truly one of the nicest human beings I've ever met. We shared our love for sports. I always enjoyed my conversations with Ken, a very intelligent man who could talk about any topic. It was obvious from the first time we met that the Yanofsky's and the Bailey's would be livelong friends.

CHAPTER SIX

Homeowners Twice Over

Let's take a break from my string of radio station conversations and talk about everyone's single most important purchase; buying a house.

I was commuting to Manchester, NH from Burlington, MA. That, my friends, was quite a schlep, and so three years into my tenure at WKBR, Paula and I decided in 1984 to buy our first home. It was a brown split level and our new address was 5 Hampton Drive in Nashua, NH, only about 25 minutes or so from the radio station. Prior to moving in, we had a meeting with the previous owners who wanted to go over different features in the house. At that time, Paula and I noticed that across the street our new neighbors still had their Christmas lights up. We thought that was rather strange since it was April. When we actually moved into our new home in May, the Christmas lights were still there. Our new neighbors were Cheryl and Bob Maguire, and they came over to welcome us. It so happened that they had been on vacation and their friends in the neighborhood pulled a prank on them. They went into the Maguire's home and brought out all of their stored

Christmas decorations and hung them on the exterior of the house. We thought that was hysterical and would eventually learn that our new neighborhood practiced pranks on a regular basis. In fact, the Maguire's would leave their Christmas lights up for a few more weeks just to torture the neighbors with their own prank.

We became very good friends with the Maguire's and their children, Karen and Rick. They were a special family and, speaking of Christmas, would always invite us into their home for the holidays for a neighborhood celebration. Christmas Eve at the Maguire's became a tradition that lasted well after we moved. Karen and Rick were wonderful to Daniel, always playing a *Star Wars* board game with him, filled with detailed trivia questions. The competition was something that Daniel would always look forward to and they treated him like their little brother.

Nine years later, I had changed jobs to go back across the border to work at WCGY/WCCM in Lawrence, MA. The job change precipitated another nerve-racking and stressful commute. So after further review we decided that a new job would translate into a new home. In addition, a move further south would mean that we'd be closer to our friends and family on the South Shore. Then in 1993, we moved to Andover, Massachusetts, only 15 minutes from my newest radio station. At the time, Andover's population was around 28,000 and had a very relaxing small town feel, as opposed to the City of Nashua with over 80,000 people. The street was filled with children close to Daniel's age, making it a nice transition for him. Plus, we had a swimming pool, a natural draw for his new buddies. Another reason we were drawn to Andover was its excellent school system.

When we got settled, I proceeded to convert my basement into a sports gallery, adding a pool table; the ultimate man cave. On the outside, we added a basketball hoop. Now, I was all set. Twenty-eight years later, we're still here and loving it!

Now let's return to the radio portion of the program……

CHAPTER SEVEN

Working for a Legend in Lawrence, Two More Fathers and Two More Radio Stations

I was 33 years young when I began my next challenge in 1986. Little did I know at the time that WCGY/WCCM in Lawrence would prove to be what I would call "the ultimate radio family."

The personable Paul Seccareccio, the station's General Manager, thankfully hired me, making 93.7 on the FM dial and Radio 800 on the AM dial, my home away from home for the next nine years. The call letters WCGY stood for Curt Gowdy, the legendary Hall of Fame sportscaster. My job was to sell radio time for both radio stations. One of the greatest moments in my life happened when I was first summoned into Curt Gowdy's massive office. I remember it like it was yesterday. He had a huge mahogany desk and pictures mounted everywhere. He wanted to meet the new hire and I certainly wanted to meet him. With his legs propped up on his desk and eating an apple at the time, I entered the sanctuary. As a side note here, I was a huge Curt Gowdy fan. When I was 20 years younger, I would sneak my transistor radio into bed at night to listen to Mr. Gowdy broadcast the Red Sox games. Curt (look at me, I'm on a first name basis) did it all when it came to sports broadcasting. Not only was he the voice of the Red Sox, but he also was the key announcer for the old American Football League. And now here I was, ready, willing and able to work for the guy! His son, Trevor, was the General Manager and his daughter, Cheryl Ann, was on-the-air as well as being the program director. I was also pretty psyched about the cool rock music that WCGY played.

It didn't take me long to meet the King of the Castle. The man that everyone looked up to and the glue that kept everyone happy together; Bruce Arnold Salvucci. Bruce was the soothing morning voice that listeners' in the Merrimack Valley woke up to every Monday through Friday. As it turned out, Bruce performed his professional schtick for over four decades. He was WCCM's program director, but titles mattered very little to him. Not something you see every day from a manager. When I met Bruce he was already half way to building his resume that would someday land him in the Massachusetts Broadcaster's Hall of Fame. He was an endearing man with an incredible sense of humor and possessed a warmth that went well beyond description.

Now Bruce didn't have what I would call a clean, well-organized office, but if you could find a place to sit down, he would always find the time to speak with you. I mean really, has there ever been a kinder man on the face of the earth than Bruce Arnold? Those that are reading this book and had the privilege of working with him know exactly what I'm talking about. Bruce always said, "If I drop this pencil, I expect that you'll pick it up for me, but when you drop your pencil, I'll be there to pick it up for you." Sounds like a simple saying, huh? No, it was more than that. He showed me that you could actually be a "nice" guy and still be an effective manager. A lesson that included how your daily actions would earn you respect, unlike so many managers that I encountered who demanded respect before earning it. My mother once said that it doesn't cost any more to be nice to people. Unknowingly I guess that Bruce and my mother were on the same page.

Bruce also taught me that people who had differences could sit down and work things out if you simply made the effort. These are just some of the attributes that made Bruce Arnold so special. And so was his family. Bruce's incredible wife, Lenora, and daughters, Lisa and Sharon, were so proud of him. They were down to earth and always pleasant, just like their dad and husband. When you think of listening to Bruce on the radio, you remember the many snowstorms that he brought his listeners through, even if it took sleeping at the radio station to make sure that everyone knew what was going on and how to be safe in the process. He gave his listeners a sense of calm, a sense of community and a ton of positive energy. "Purely Personal, the WCCM Backyard BBQ's" were just a few of Bruce's finest moments.

The WCCM Backyard BBQ's was one of the best local promotions that I can remember. Listeners would mail in a postcard in the hopes that Bruce would choose them to win the grand prize. You and 50 guests would be treated to an incredible BBQ in your own backyard hosted by the staff of WCCM and WCGY.

We did all the cooking. Bruce would give his customary speech at the BBQ, introducing our staff. Talk about warm and fuzzy. And the food was damn good!

Bruce Arnold and John Bassett, my second and third fathers

Then there was the silver fox, otherwise known as J.B., John Bassett, another one of those guys that you just wanted to be around. John was another person at Curt Gowdy Broadcasting who I attached myself to and loved every minute of it. I remember that every morning, JB would dive into the *Boston Globe* and read the paper from cover to cover. Then, on a weekly basis, was off to his Rotary Club meeting. JB served as the General Manager of Curt Gowdy Broadcasting and had been a friend of the family for many years. He was a huge sports fan and that's why we clicked so well. John worked in the broadcast industry for a remarkable 57 years! JB had worked with some of the finest names in the industry and shared a microphone with Frank Avruch (of Bozo fame), Carl DeSuze, Alan Dary, Bill Marlowe, Johnny Most, Don Gillis, Bill Harrington, Fred

Cusick and Ken Coleman. He was chosen to be the program director in the 1960's for WHDH AM/FM. JB was also the driving force who developed the very first roundtable sports talk show on the radio. JB did it all and I believe that he's more than worthy as an inductee to the Massachusetts Broadcasters Hall of Fame. We had that conversation when he was 91 years old. He told me that would be great and I promised him that someday he would be there. On his death bed not too long after that I repeated my promise. I will not break that promise.

We had many unique and talented personalities at WCCM. Wily veteran Billy Curtin was one of the best at sharing stories and jokes to everyone he met. Never a dull moment with Billy and I so much enjoyed our crazy conversations. Everyone's good friend Mark Hobbs did the most hilarious impression of Billy Curtin. It was hysterical! Other memorable characters included the great Mark Mitchell, the quintessential old school professional sales guy who always offered his help and sometimes even sales leads. Milt Kray was the national sales manager and was one of the wisest men I ever met. Again, mild-mannered but could always get his point across succinctly and would drop everything to help you.

Frank Benjamin, the man about town and local sports guru was someone I liked right off the bat. Two very special ladies were Gene Silver who I had met at my first radio station and who trained me to be a bookkeeper, and Pat Johnson, who served as Curt Gowdy's personal secretary for many years. Gene put everyone in their place and never pulled any punches. She had a wonderful sense of humor and it was so easy to speak with her about any subject. Pat was calm, collected, quiet but again, someone that would love to engage in a conversation. Pat is a very special lady. Add office worker Ollie into the mix and it all meant that the office was in good hands. Lucky for them that I wasn't a part of that department.

As I've said, Bruce Arnold led the way for sure, but he had a strong crew that always got the job done. Bob Schufrieder and Ben Mevorach in the news department, Joe Souci, the engineer, John Moran, a talk show master, Danny Roche, the sports guy, who would later on become a mainstay at WBZ-TV, and Jimi Carter who was Bruce's right hand man and did just about everything. When you work at WCGY/WCCM, your immediate family became part of the radio family. It always went smoothly. We didn't have to stop and take notice of who was at the events and why. It was a given, it was accepted and everyone just wanted to help. Again no doubt that Bruce Arnold had a lot to do with that. Bruce could also be referred to as a master matchmaker. He was indirectly or directly responsible for several marriages that blossomed at 33 Franklin Street in Lawrence. Now how about the other side of the building? Yes, the craziness and the lovefest continued at WCGY 93.7.

WCGY 93.7 went from The Rock Garden to Superhits (with a Superman logo) to Classic Hits from the start of my tenure in 1986 until the time the station was sold. Thinking back, this is where the party started and never ended. I have a huge smile on my face as I type this special section.

Paul Seccareccio was incredible at putting together great sales staffs. He was like a baseball manager figuring out what players would make for good chemistry in the clubhouse. Cheryl Healey, from the valley made a very good sales manager and was a hard-working and personable sales woman. She was very nice to me and all her clients loved her for sure. Maria Farrah, Nancy DiSalvo, Cynthia Owens, Kathy Rodwell, Connie O'Donnell, Chris Barber and Jennifer Long are all worth mentioning. Simply good people and a lot of fun to work with. Then there was Mark Hobbs and Sam Uvino. Call us the

Three Musketeers or if you'd prefer, The Three Stooges. Hobbs and Uvino were master sales guys and pretty damn good musicians and singers as well!

WCGY had an extremely successful morning show. Ownership never invested in Arbitron ratings books but we knew that we had a good thing going. Mike Morin was the star of stars. He was creative and sharp with an incredible sense of humor. Along with Mike, the morning show consisted of producer Steve Gamlin, talented sidekick Gary Leavitt. Dan Roche and Bob Schufrieder would come over from the AM side to deliver the sports and the news. When Danny left for the big time, he was replaced by the talented John Vitale. John also worked as the track announcer at Rockingham Park in Salem, NH.

Back to the morning show. When there was any listener interaction requested, the phones lit up. Mike Morin was a showman and constantly came up with crazy ideas to entertain the listeners. One of the craziest and press worthy schticks that Mike and his team came up with was three "buried alive" promotions. Yes, he was actually "buried alive" and gave a play-by-play description to his loyal listeners. The promotions went like this as described by Mike.

Buried Alive 1 – At Bliss Marine in Woburn. I was nailed into a wooden coffin-like box for 48 hours where I broadcast my show live (not dead) one morning. I spent my down time reading the new Johnny Carson bio. I was buried under a pile of recyclable trash to call attention to the environment. My 9-year old daughter was horrified.

Buried Alive 2 - At Jim Witt Pontiac in Lowell. I spent 48-hours in a 5,000-pound block of ice to raise money for Special Olympics. Doctor Silkini hypnotized me again so that I could remain alive while wearing only shorts and a T inside the massive ice cube.

Buried Alive - 3 At Spooky World in Berlin. It happened a few weeks after Gowdy sold the station. My show producer Steve Gamlin dutifully stood guard each night while Tiny Tim sang his repertoire of falsetto songs on the adjacent stage as patrons cued up for the haunted hayride.

Every time I think I'm ready to move on to another radio station, I'm reminded of more co-workers that need to be recognized.

Brad Hallenborg made sure that our radio station appearances went flawless and is truly a genuine guy. Steve Gamlin, the producer of the Mike Morin show, "Morin in the Morning," wore multiple hats as a copywriter and production guy. Gary Leavitt, the man with 1000 voices, did a mean impression of Celtic announcer Johnny Most. In fact, Mrs. Most told Gary that his impression of her husband was the best she ever heard! Julie Deveraux, Kimberly Jaeger and Lisa Garvey were on the air, along with Spider Spence, Jerry (Duke of Madness) Goodwin, who later on became quite an accomplished actor, and the likeable Harvey Warfield. A ton of talent under the roof of one radio station. All of this happened in nine years, but there's more.

When it comes to radio, you certainly meet some the best people. When the day ends however, most people go home. WCGY was different. Whether it was gathering at Leo's Pub in Lawrence to sing karaoke, play softball and join WCCM for their backyard BBQ promotions, we were together often.

A word about the softball team. We called ourselves the WCGY Rock Sox. I was the self-appointed coach. I loved writing out the line-ups, just like Red Sox skipper Joe Morgan did in 1990. My most dependable and maybe only pitcher was Mike Morin. I don't know if Mike got his smooth pitching motion from his experience as a championship candlepin bowler, but the guy could throw strikes. Everything else was a juggling act since I really didn't know who was going to show up. On the air, Mike would challenge local teams to a game of co-ed softball. The games were a blast. Most notable hitters on the Rock Sox were Danny Roche, who seemed to hit the ball over the fence just about every other at-bat. Steve (the Ramblin' Man) had a big stick as well and was usually the clean-up hitter. Mark Hobbs could hit the ball a country mile. Pam Roche is quite an athlete and she impressed us all every time she made an appearance on the diamond. Sean Sullivan was our best left fielder and Trevor Gowdy could also whack the ball a long way and had a rocket for an arm. I actually kept the statistics at the games (anyone surprised?), filled out the line-up card and played first base. I loved playing that position. In reality, where else was a lefty going to play on the diamond? Not many shortstops or second basemen are left-handed. I definitely preferred first than chasing balls in the outfield. An earlier version of Steve enjoyed that, but not the WCGY version.

Later on during my WCGY nine-year tenure, I would become the local sales manager. Veteran radio programming guy Jim Murphy served as the station GM at that time. We clicked very well with mutual goals to keep the sales momentum going. We always strived to develop a staff that blended well together. The same kind of chemistry that was well-established by Paul Seccareccio and Cheryl Healey. It was a pretty good job for me. Imagine a sales management position where the owner or General Manager doesn't give you a budget to achieve? So that meant less stress and when 6:00 pm rolled around, I was writing up the softball team's line-up.

Unfortunately, the station was sold in 1994 to American Radio and like a scene from *Fiddler on the Roof*, everyone had to leave their home away from home and go in different directions. I wish that never happened. I'd probably still be there if it hadn't.

In 2010, I hosted a WCGY/WCCM reunion. It was a very special day. Mrs. Gowdy and her daughter, Cheryl Ann, made sure that the party was a success! They even provided the incredible food. Cheryl Ann used her designer talents to make my backyard look the best it's ever been.

My good-bye message to the best radio family ever, 1994

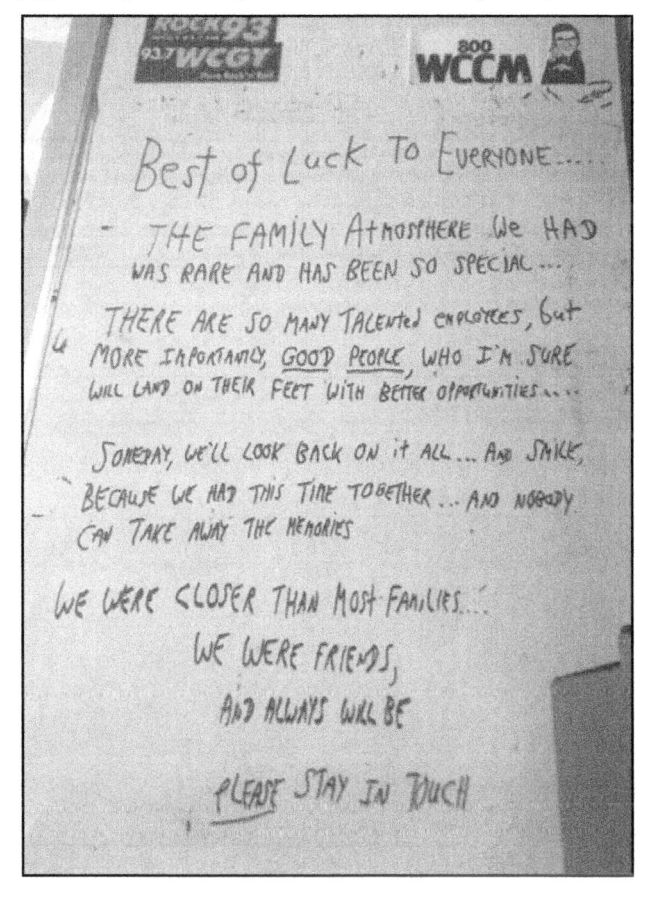

> Best of Luck To Everyone....
>
> - THE FAMILY Atmosphere We HAD WAS RARE AND HAS BEEN SO SPECIAL...
>
> THERE ARE SO MANY TALENTED employees, but MORE IMPORTANTLY, GOOD PEOPLE, WHO I'M SURE WILL LAND ON THEIR FEET WITH BETTER OPPORTUNITIES.....
>
> SOMEDAY, WE'LL LOOK BACK ON it ALL... AND SMILE, BECAUSE WE HAD THIS TIME TOGETHER... AND NOBODY CAN TAKE AWAY THE MEMORIES
>
> WE WERE CLOSER THAN MOST FAMILIES...
>   WE WERE FRIENDS,
>   AND ALWAYS WILL BE
>
> PLEASE STAY IN TOUCH

Very few staffers missed this event. It was classic!

Daniel on the WCGY motorcycle

Mark Mitchell, Tracey, Jennifer and Sam working at the WCCM BBQ promotion. Now that's what I call teamwork!

CHAPTER EIGHT

WSSH-ing to Make a Lot of Dough

Throughout my 41-year radio career, I've been lucky to have the opportunity to work with some pretty good sales managers. Some pretty lousy ones as well. Well, I was about to meet one of the very best.

In 1995, I got a call from the sales manager of a very popular radio station. It was WSSH-FM and a guy named Joe DiDonato. I loved his style and approach to the broadcast industry. He was a pretty cool dude and I was thrilled when he offered me the opportunity to sell radio time at WSSH 99.5. It helped that they had such a great reputation in the Boston market. The studios and offices were located at Soldiers Field Road in Boston. We shared the building with staffers from WBOS.

Here's a little history about the 50,000-watt powerhouse known as WSSH-FM, well before I got there. Boston's 'WISH', was all about playing beautiful music. If you liked Percy Faith, Perry Como and Doris Day, it didn't get any better than WSSH-FM in Lowell. While WJIB 96.9 "Boston Talks' reigned as the king of "muzak," WSSH outlasted other beautiful music stations like WCOZ 94.5 and WBOS 92.9. The automated beautiful music station probably benefited most from a better mix of "elevator" music, good sounding announcers and a strong signal. For some reason, everything sounded good on the 99.5 dial position. Most of the instrumental music faded in the early 1980s, giving way to more of an adult contemporary format, featuring familiar artists like John Denver, Neil Diamond, Anne Murray and the Carpenters. The 50,000-watt presentation of soothing sounds really came into its own, however, in the late 80's when WSSH moved to Woburn and featured some fantastic live local talent, especially Jordan Rich. Today, Rich is well known as a talk show host on WBZ-AM. Eventually, smooth jazz, country music (WKLB) and classical music (WCRB) would have their turns at 99.5 on the FM radio dial.

Let me say a word or two about WSSH. I never worked for WSSH when it was in Lowell, but its reputation as the hip adult contemporary radio station gave me a fantastic product to sell. Jordan Rich was established in the radio community as a top-notch morning personality. Susan Rosenberg was the talented program director.

Now here's a radio story for the ages. Our office manager was a great lady named Louise Sullivan. She had another side to her that I wasn't aware of until the second half of my stint at WSSH. Louise was a certified WITCH! You heard me right. No, not even close to the *Wizard of Oz's* Wicked Witch of the West. Louise was closer to Elizabeth Montgomery's witch on the popular TV sitcom, *Bewitched.*

Well, one day after a sales call I returned to the radio station around 2:00 pm. For some reason the building was dark. I thought that maybe the station was sold and no one told me. As I entered the sales area, the room was filled with candles and a ton of station personnel. I said out loud, "Hey what's going on?" Several people quickly told me to be quiet. It so happens that Louise was doing an exorcism on one of the sales desks! The desk in question always seemed to be inhabited by an unsuccessful sales person. Maybe you could call it jinxed. So why not do an exorcism and rid the desk of evil spirits? Seemed like the right thing to do at the time. Bet you never heard that one before.

Unfortunately, the station's ratings declined. They tried to revive it by calling it the "New WSSH." Insider information told me that the only change they made was eliminating Kenny

Rogers and Barbra Streisand from its playlist. It didn't work. I was still selling to my loyal clients until one day during our weekly sales meeting we would be thrown for a loop. Joe and the station's General Manager, John Laton, ran the meeting and revealed what was to happen next. John and Joe said that they had something very exciting to announce. They explained to the sales staff that the company had done extensive research on the music scene in Boston. At that point they actually ripped off their dress shirts and revealed a new and strange looking tee shirt. It read, "The Oasis." It was determined that the next popular format in Boston would be 'smooth jazz.' Really? The reaction in the room was shocking, surprising and downright negative. WSSH would become "The Oasis." Oh boy, just when I was building quite an account list and making some good change.

I remember meeting with one of my best seasonal clients, Wayne Ulaky, owner of Canobie Lake Park in Salem, NH. Wayne was a jazz aficionado and when I presented the new format he said to me, "Steve this isn't jazz, it's a whiney sax featuring Kenny G. That's not my customer. Thanks but no thanks. I'll have to pass." At that moment I thought to myself, maybe I should pass as well…..to another radio station. I think of WSSH before the change as WMJX is today. WSSH and MAGIC were both adult contemporary music formats and extremely popular with a large devoted audience. They simply existed in two different eras. One good thing that came out of WSSH was Jordan Rich, who would later become a client and more importantly, a friend. His agency, Chart Productions, handled some great accounts, most notably the Boston Pops. Jordan also put his voice to all of the Sullivan Tire commercials. His partner, Ken Carberry, was equally as nice and extremely knowledgeable about the industry, especially since his family had many years of experience in the field. Chart Productions was located in the Statler Building in Boston and later on moved to an office/studio in Braintree. MA. Jordan and I both graduated Randolph High School, just a few years apart. We have a yearly tradition of getting together for lunch at Legal Seafood. Good company, good food and good times. I hope that this tradition continues despite my retirement from the radio game.

CHAPTER NINE

W-R-O-R.....Wish I Could Pronounce My 'R's

As I pondered my next sales job, I was fortunate that I didn't have to wait too long. I got a call from Rick Alpern,, the new sales manager for WROR-FM 105.7. From what I remember, WROR had left the airwaves for a couple of years and then made a triumphant return. Rick was building a sales team and I was the lucky one that he chose first. The radio station was a part of Greater Media. Other stations included in the group were WMJX (Magic), WBOS, WCLB, which later became WKLB and WSJZ, that would become talk station WTTK. I kind of liked working with a group of five radio stations. After all, that meant five times the people.

For the first year we were located at the Prudential Building in Boston, sharing the office with the WCLB folks. WMJX and WBOS were just a few blocks away on Stuart Street. It was pretty cool being in the Pru, eating lunch on Newbury Street, watching the hustle and bustle of people in the big city and simply feeling that I had hit the big time. In addition they gave me a parking pass in a garage so I didn't have to worry about meter maids again. It turned out that the Pru was just a temporary landing place and pretty soon we would all be moving to Morrissey Boulevard a few miles further south of the city. It was also located right next door to the *Boston Globe*. Before the move, Jeff Messerman (may he rest in peace) and I had decided to check out the new place. The carpenters were banging away at the wooden planks and it wasn't easy getting around the building. Obviously, the facility that would house five radio stations and their employees was still in its infancy stages. Nonetheless, I got a first- hand look of what would be my new workplace for the next eight years. After almost one year at the Prudential Center, my new work address would become 55 Morrissey Boulevard. The sales area consisted of one gigantic room, made up of six rows of cubicles for the sales staff. On the perimeter were the offices of the sales managers. Around the corner were the WROR, WMJX, WBOS, WKLB and the WSJZ studios, all adjacent to each other. It was referred to as broadcast row. My new radio family was humungous. Each sales staff averaged about seven sales people. Add to that their respective sales managers, program directors, promotion directors, on-air staff, production crew and interns, all who would reside on the second floor of a two- story building. On the first floor, the receptionists, the personable David Aucoin and the always pleasant Gwen greeted the station's visitors. You would also find the office and financial staff on the bottom floor. Overall, it was a beautiful and expansive facility.

When it came to upper management, the prominent names were Matt Mills, Annie McGuire and Alan Chartrand. They worked in conjunction with each station's sales managers and program directors to ensure that the group as a whole would be successful.

One of the more popular shows within our group of stations was the Loren and Wally morning show starring Loren Owens and Wally Brine. The two of them joined forces in 1981 at WVBF in Framingham and then in 1982 at WROR. The dynamic duo stayed together until 2016 when Wally retired. Loren continued the program until his retirement in 2019. That's 38 years of entertaining throngs of listeners throughout New England. Very, very impressive and that longevity was extremely rare. They certainly were the lifeblood of the radio station and their ratings remained strong throughout the years.

The morning show also included the many talents of Tom Doyle. Tom produced a very entertaining CD called "Tom's Townie Tunes." If any of you out there would like a copy, simply get in touch with me. I know I kept extras. The production was a take-off on various cities and towns in Massachusetts set to popular songs of the day. For example, "Mattapan Again," was a take-off of Willie Nelson's "On the Road Again." Then there was "All You Need is Lunch," Tom's version of the Beatles "All You Need is Love." One of my favorites was "These Boots Were Made in Brockton," from Nancy Sinatra's "These Boots Were Made For Walking."

Brian Bell was the producer of the show, Sue provided the news and the loveable Hank Morse provided the traffic reports as well as being the "talent" at several of my promotional appearances. I remember that Hank and I survived an appearance on a "gambling cruise" called Horizon's Edge. It sailed out of Revere and was certainly one of the more unique "appearances" I've ever encountered. Hank was a pro in every sense of the word and of course the crowd loved him. I think I played a little blackjack and came out even, which for me is a big win!

One of the more popular features was Loren and Wally's "Men from Maine." Another fan favorite was Bob Ryan, referred to by Loren as "Mr. Everything." Ryan, a long time

Globe sports reporter, provided his insight in the world of sports, as the morning team would spearhead the conversation. I had campaigned for the "Bob Ryan Report" for a while and was so happy when it became a long-time feature on the show.

WROR was a fun station to sell. So many promotions and "live" broadcasts throughout New England. As an account rep, I was always searching for ways to tie my clients into the fabric of the radio station. My best connection came when I tied my largest client, Dunkin' Donuts, with the Loren and Wally show. There was no doubt that the slogan "America Runs on Dunkin" was true, but more importantly you could say that the "Yanofsky Family Runs on Dunkin!" Dunkin' Donuts would become my largest account for the next twenty years. I would receive gift certificates from Dunkin's field manager Shannon Maxwell, give them to Brian Bell, who would then buy the products and feed them to Loren and Wally.

The dynamic duo would then talk about the products on the air in what was referred to as a "live" endorsement. It worked well, Dunkin' was pleased and so was I. The commissions I received from Dunkin' kept pouring in as I enjoyed feasting on their products. My favorites included their iced coffee and their glazed donuts.

Great co-workers were plentiful during my nine years at Greater Media. Some of them are pictured below.

One of my all-time favorite co-workers was Judy Weinberg. We shared many a lunch together. She was a phenomenal sales person and still is today in the real estate market. Judy and I even share the same birthday, May 30.

Bottom row: Jeff Messerman, Janet Haley, Jen Bousquet, Kerry Ann Simbron and Judy Weinberg, Top row: Paul Sullivan and me with my mouth wide open as usual.

As I mentioned, any great radio family must have a softball team. Greater Media did as well. We actually played in the Boston Media League. The games were played in the softball fields behind Harvard University. We were led by Annie McGuire, who was by far our best pitcher. Heidi Strasnick stood out as an enthusiastic cheerleader, but also a solid hitter and fielder. The crazy part was that five or six games would be played simultaneously next to each other. As I played first base, the left fielder of another game would be very close behind me. It wasn't the ideal situation. What was ideal was that following the games we would all head to the Bucket, a popular pub in Watertown and put down a few pitchers of beer. Winning or losing really didn't matter at that point. How many pitchers of beer we needed was the important question. These were definitely some of the most memorable times that further strengthened the bond of the Greater Media family.

I'd be remiss if I didn't mention some of my closer Greater Media friends like my next door cubicle buddy Matt DiRoberto. It was Matt's first radio job and he picked it up pretty quickly. During my time at WROR, I watched him grow into a super salesman and more importantly a great family man. His success was rewarded later on when he was named WROR's sales manager. Jeannine Randolph, who worked for Magic was a very talented account executive. We shared some great times in and around Boston. Rick Alpern, who I had admired greatly, was definitely one of the best sales managers that I ever had the pleasure of working with. To this day, we're still good friends and have followed each other's careers and families for over 30 years. Rick even invites me as his guest to see Boston Bruins games. Joe Derry, a former client of mine at Haffner's Oil, is also a part of the B's party. Good times and really good people.

CHAPTER TEN

14 Years of Rollin' on the River

My longest tenure at any radio station began in 2004 and lasted all the way to 2017. Fourteen years I spent at WXRV 92.5 the River. That means 14 years of memories. For the purpose of this book, the River deserves many pages.

I started my "River" career in 2004. Yes, that special year when the Boston Red Sox broke the "curse" and won their first World Series in 86 years. None of that really mattered to the station's owner, Steven Silberberg. He was a passionate man. Passionate about his radio stations, his farm in Bedford, NH. and of course, his family. Steven owned several radio stations across the country, from Wyoming to Vermont, but WXRV/92.5 was his favorite and number-one breadwinner. As an independent broadcast owner, he created a unique "family" atmosphere. In this case the word "unique" is an understatement.

As I said Steven was passionate and also very involved in the day to day operations of his properties. When you work with someone for 14 years, you certainly see the good, the bad and the ugly. Steven had high expectations for everyone around him and could be a real tiger. But inside, he was more like a pussycat and possessed a very good heart. He gave many of us the opportunity to flourish in the crazy world of radio and created an atmosphere that was void of the corporate world. Clear Channel, Entercom, Greater Media and others were the big shots in Boston. WXRV/92.5 was the distinct underdog, but was more than able to hold its place as a popular regional radio station with over 400,000 weekly fanatical and diehard fans. The River featured a talented staff of on-air personalities and salespeople that could compete against the best of them. I was hired to be the local sales manager and worked alongside general manager Bob Mendelsohn. Bob had a lengthy career in radio and had been the national sales manager at WBCN. Bob and I hit it off very quickly and did everything we could to please the big guy, whose corporate office was in Bedford, NH.

Bob was patient and very smart and we made a very good team together.

We had a unique cast of characters to deal with, yet still made it work. I was very big into the chemistry of the sales team, one that could work well together and produce the sales numbers that we were looking for. That was a lesson that I learned from previous managers. Sort of like a baseball manager who could develop a well-oiled team with a positive clubhouse atmosphere. It was never easy but the day-to-day challenge was always intriguing to me.

Within the ancient walls of 92.5 The River was a legendary studio converted into a mini concert venue and many of us referred to it as the famous River Music Hall. One of the perks of the job was attending these incredible and intimate performances along with River listeners. The room could comfortably fit 50 guests; any more was stretching it a bit. Some of the bigger names included Graham Nash and David Crosby, Ziggy Marley, Ed Sheeran, Adele, John Mayer, Coldplay, Imagine Dragons, Tori Amos, Grace Potter, Guster, Billy Idol, Jason Mraz, Ingrid Michaelson, Barenaked Ladies,

Scars on 45, Adam Ezra group and Delta Rae, Coldplay, John Mayer, F.U.N., The Lumineers, and Squeeze.

Ziggy Marley in the River Music Hall

I continue my 'River' chapter with a song I wrote to the tune of Bobby Darin's "Mack the Knife." circa 2010.

Oh there's a station, down 495, called the River, they used it call it Lite.
Just a stone's throw from downtown Haverhill and the building is quite a site.
I want to tell ya, bout the River, babe,
It keep's growing and it's startin' to spread
And the sales staff, they hit their numba's (sometimes)

So there's nevah, nevah a trace of red.
Now in the a.m., every weekday mornin,
There's Dana Marshall, just a soundin' fine (ay!)
Playin' great tunes for 400,000,
Just to make them, forget the traffic grind.
There's Carolyn Morrell (hup, hup, hup) mid-days on the river don't you know,
Playin' picnic lunch tunes and she's getting on down.
Then in pm drive playin' five o'clock shadow, no doubt that's Matty, that's right Matty's back in town.
Now, did you hear about Johny Mullett? He works 24 hours a day babe, running around the River, trying to make some cash.
You should hear him jamming on his fender and in the prize closet, he keeps the River's stash.
Now, now Steven Friedman, oh, oh, yeah Jackie Frary, ooh miss Cindy G. and the famous Doremus too. Oh, Montezinos, AJ,, Gary and that's me, Steve Young. I'm just swingin' and singin' this tune.
I said Irene, Pippins, Lindsay, and Dana, whoa Donald and Steven, look out Kimmy and Jenna, they're playing in traffic downtown. Yes the party starts at 30 Howe Street, babe. Now that the River's got the sound.... Look out the river is back!

When it comes to radio formats, the River was not the easiest to define and sometimes a bit challenging for the sales staff, especially when we had to describe the format to people who were unfamiliar with the station. A sports talk station, talks about sports. A country station plays country music. A news station features the news. No explanation is needed in those cases. My presentation and description of the music we played changed slightly from year to year. It was referred to in radio circles as Adult Album Alternative or Triple A. That didn't really mean anything to clients. In a nutshell, the River is an adult rock radio station that plays a diverse mix of music. Music from the 60's and 70's, classic rock, alternative bands from the 80's and 90's and even singer-songwriters were included in the mix. Then, the salespeople would give specific examples of some of the more popular artists. The River was a station like no other and offered something on the radio dial that no one else dared to do. That was our niche and Steven Silberberg never wanted to stray from that unique mix of music.

There were plenty of key players at 30 How Street in Haverhill, but none as special in the early days at the River as Steve Adolphson. When you look up "gentleman" in the dictionary, you would see a picture of Steve. He worked at the River for 27 years and was well-liked by everyone who met him. He was soft spoken but very smart and kind. I enjoyed our time together, and we always had great conversations about sales and life. I was extremely fortunate to have had the pleasure to meet him and work with him.

Steve squared----
Steven S. and Steve A.

Silberberg and I did go bike-riding together once in Boston. He wasn't nuts about the route I took him on, but it was quite an adventure. We started adjacent to the Charles River next to Storrow Drive and then looped around to the Cambridge side of the river. Steven was doing his best at navigating his antiquated bicycle. I had a pretty decent and fairly new hybrid bike. About halfway around the Charles River I thought that if we switched bikes Steven would enjoy the bike ride a lot more. He agreed and took off rather quickly leaving me in the dust. I got stuck at a busy intersection while Steven did his best Evel Knievel impression by weaving in and out between the moving vehicles as fast as he could....with my bike, of course. When I finally caught up to him our bike trip continued as we headed towards Faneuil Hall. The next stop would be lunch at Joe's American Bar & Grill. As we ordered our meal, Steven considered a fish platter and proceeded to ask the poor waiter where did the fish come from? The perplexed young waiter said that he'd ask the chef. Upon his return, the waiter tried to avoid the question and take our order. Well, if you know Steven then you know that wasn't going to happen. Finally the waiter said that neither he nor the chef knew where the fish came from. Maybe he just should've said the Atlantic Ocean. Steven raised his voice slightly and couldn't understand why the chef didn't know. He ordered the fish dinner anyways, added clam chowder and all was well.

We had a great conversation about our next bike ride and that he would definitely go and purchase a brand new bicycle for himself. We never did ride again but that experience was vintage Steven.

Riding our bikes alongside the Charles River

My favorite "Steven" story was definitely our trip to Fenway Park to see Paul McCartney in concert. Accompanied by our wives, we parked about a half-mile away from B.U. and headed to Fenway. All of a sudden Steven stopped and said, "Wait here, I have to go into this building." It was his college dormitory when he was a student at B.U. Well, the dorm was locked, but Steven insisted on waiting until someone would let him in. He went around the side of the building and we didn't see him again for another half-hour. As it turned out, he finagled his way into the dorm and went to his old dorm room from years ago. According to his account of the story, he had quite a conversation with several students. Paul McCartney would have to wait for us!

Never a dull moment working at the River, especially in the early years. Bob Stuart was a mid-day fixture with a distinctive and pleasant voice. Steve Adolphson, Steve Friedman, Bill Phenix, Bonnie Cartwright, Cindy Griswold, Lynne Fiske, Dennis Hennessey, Mark McKeller, Sue Cate, Fred Ford, and Don LeBrun made up my sales team. If I left you out, then please let me know and I'll buy you lunch. Jay Lufkin was the production director and very good at his craft, and Catie Wilbur became the program director. The wonderful Dana Marshall was the AM drive-time announcer. Lisa Garvey and Patty Fox were on-air personalities (we stopped calling them jocks in those days) and they were both talented and extremely knowledgeable about the music we played.

By that point of my career, I had been in broadcast sales for 25 years. That meant that I had developed my own style of management, was confident in my approach, and knew exactly how I would proceed when it came to running the sales side of the building. With all that said, I had one big challenge ahead of me. Some say it was a good challenge, others said that it was a negative. Most likely it was somewhere in the middle. The challenge was separating myself from being someone's friend and their boss at the same time. It was like walking a tightrope and hoping not to fall or in this case, fail. When a salesperson came into my office to spill their guts about a personal problem, it was difficult for me to avoid helping them. I learned pretty quickly that I had to draw the line sooner or later. It was probably later, but the bottom line was that we made it work and sales continued to grow during my tenure as sales manager. From my WCCM days, I learned from the master, Bruce Arnold that it was possible to be a nice guy and still be an effective manager. Thanks Bruce.

To clearly describe what my expectations were I created the following..

'The Seventeen Commandments of Sales'

1. **FOCUS** everyday on how you can close new and old business.

2. **ORGANIZE** each week and day to set yourself up for winning

3. Be **PROMPT** for every sales meeting, every client meeting

4. Dress and act **PROFESSIONALLY** at all times

5. Be **ENTHUSIASTIC**.....it's infectious

6. Be **PASSIONATE** about your product

7. **STRIVE** to become a **SUSTAINING RESOURCE** for your clients

8. Be **OPEN** to new ideas, don't be afraid of change, it's a good thing

9. Be **PREPARED** to become a better salesperson today than you were yesterday

10. Be **CONFIDENT** in your abilities, you're better than you think

11. Treat your support staff with **RESPECT**...treat them like gold, they can make you look very good or very bad

12. Work **HARD**, but more importantly, work **SMART**

13. **READ, READ, READ....knowledge is POWER**

14. Be **POSITIVE** when at work, leave your problems at home

15. **GRAB** this wonderful opportunity to better your financial position

16. **COMMUNICATE**...we're in the communications business

17. **LAUGH** at any jokes that Steven or Steve may tell, even if it's not funny

So in my humble opinion, what does it take to be a successful person? All of the above for sure, but in a few words it takes **ENTHUSIAM, LOVE OF YOUR PRODUCT, LOVE OF WHAT YOU'RE DOING, PASSION** (one of my favorite words) and how much you **CARE** about the people around you, your co-workers and clients. Selling radio time is not an easy job, however if you master these elements then you'll most likely be successful.

ROLLIN ON THE RIVER.....A POEM FOR THE HOLIDAYS

Twas the night before Christmas and all through the station, all the salespeople were smiling, looking forward to their holiday vacation.

Trisch was cleaning up and making her desk clean, while Hannah was closing another deal and so was Marlene.

You know when it comes to radio sales, our world is wacky; But there's one person that handles it well and that's my roommate, the vivacious Jackie.

In Manchester, Friedman was spreading good cheer throughout the Granite State, Wrapping up 2011, a year for him that was even better than great!

Yes Friedman works a 70-hour week, that's true, but how could he have done it, if it weren't for the indispensable Sue!

With Catie, I share a wish when it comes to the personal people meter; That thousands will tune in to Lisa, AJ and the morning star Rita.

So Santa, played by Steven handed out gifts to his entire staff....There would be holiday cheer and everyone would enjoy a really good holiday laugh.

Wishing that 2012 will be a great year for all and hope that under your Christmas tree, you'll get a huge gift certificate from the Simon Mall.

And finally in closing, I'd like to leave you with this little insight... Treat each other how you'd like to be treated and to all a good night.

I can't emphasize enough what made the River so special. Being a local, homegrown station separate from the corporate world was something that you simply couldn't take for granted. There were no corporate offices in another part of the country. No red tape. No elaborate chain of command or political baloney. When a decision needed to be made in sales, they would come into my office, explain their position, then I would call Steven and in a heartbeat the problem would be solved. Steven Silberberg built the River that way. He also wasn't hung up on titles. You could call yourself anything you wanted to, just as long as you did your job to the best of your ability and in sales that meant bring in the dough.

It's certainly not easy to include everyone you worked with in this book. I would however, like to recognize those I worked with for a longer period of time and got to know them quite well. I think they know me pretty well, too.

Heading the list for me in sales was the sister that I never had, Trisch Doremus. She was absolutely my best hire, a terrific salesperson, extremely intelligent and more importantly a good friend. Trisch and I spent countless hours talking about our challenges in sales and in life. She's a special human being and I really miss working with her. Trisch and I are also KENO buddies!

Lindsay Burrill was the promotions director. Lindsay is the little sister that I never had. She's also one of the best athletes I've ever played with. We played basketball, ping pong, wallyball and billiards together. Even though I'm a similar age to her father and about 35 years older, she showed me NO mercy on the basketball court! She was as competitive as I am, if that's possible and defensively would stick to me like glue to prevent me from scoring. She also possesses an incredible outside jump shot. I watched Lindsay develop her talents in sales as well as her dedication as the River's Promotions Director. More importantly, she now has two precious daughters, Rosalie and Willow, along with her very cool husband, Zach.

AJ Crozby serves as the indispensable production director and on-air personality at the River. AJ is a pretty good basketball player but his on-air talents are immeasurable. When I was in sales, I would request that he put his voice onto ALL my clients radio commercials. One more thing about AJ. He's a super guy who has been the best at keeping in touch with me since I left the station. Talented, focused, intelligent and caring, that's AJ in a nutshell. BTW, his wife Amy is a gem and we share a passion for ice cream and waffle cones.

Charlie Hackett worked with me in sales as well. But, Charlie's real claim to fame is his work as an announcer. Charlie is one of the most creative people I've ever met and possesses a fantastic radio voice. He also has two incredible children, Audrey and Nathaniel. Both of them put their talents to work on a few of my radio commercials. Charlie went onto fame and I hope fortune as an on-air personality at Sirius radio.

Marlene Pippins is an excellent salesperson whose clients absolutely love her. She believes in the same approach as I did, which is developing and nurturing solid client relationships. She was certainly one of Steven Silberberg's favorites. Marlene also was a member of the beach club at one of my favorite beaches, Singing Beach located in Manchester-by-the Sea. Marlene invited us as her guests and we got the V.I.P. treatment. It's a beautiful local beach in case you've never been there.

Dennis Finn also worked in sales at the River and later on we'd work together again at my last radio station, Valley 98.9 in Methuen. Dennis had extensive sales experience, works very hard and is truly a pro's pro. We still keep in touch and I'm very happy to call him a good friend. His better half, Janet, keeps him in check.

Steve Friedman is legendary. Everyone in Southern New Hampshire knows Steve Friedman. He's a tireless worker that loves what he does. He and I would be highly competitive when it came to being the top sales dog. I think that Steven liked that.

I guess you could say that we pushed each other in a positive way. Steve's wife Darleen is definitely his better half.

Jackie Frary is a sweetheart. She has a big heart and has had lots of success in sales. Jackie is also a tremendous athlete. She's an avid skier and top notch bicyclist. We also played tennis together. Jackie's pretty damn good at that game as well.

Matt Phipps was the very able program director of the radio station. His door was always open and he developed a super relationship with all the salespeople. Matt's a devoted family man as well with his fantastic wife, Heather, and their great son, Dom.

Carolyn Morrell was our mid-day announcer. Highly talented and intelligent with a soothing voice. We worked together at a number of River appearances at North Shore Music Theatre (my all-time favorite client.). I LOVE musicals! Carolyn, by the way, also possesses a fantastic singing voice and is quite a tennis and ping pong player. She surprised me at my retirement party by writing and singing a song especially for me to the tune of Sinatra's "When I was Seventeen." No one had ever done that for me before. Here it is…

It Was a Very Good Year

by Carolyn Morrell

When he was seventeen, it was a very good year,
It was a very good year for Randolph High and their basketball team;
Steve's taller than he seems,
He ran track-and he was lean,
When he was seventeen.

When he was twenty-three, post Boston University,
It was a very good year with Miss Paula Ernest.
They'd see films and play gin, mini golf and she'd win;
He found love and felt glee, when he was twenty-three.

When he was thirty- five, it was a very good year.
He worked at CGY; he adored all those guys;
And Daniel came home;
They all said shalom.
Steve's young son had arrived,
When he was thirty-five.

When he was fifty one, it was a VERY good year for Lowe,
Ortiz and Pedro!
Their biggest fan, don't you know,
Steve prayed for the Sox,
Over bagels and lox.
Series finally won!!

When he was fifty-one.

When Steve was 59, it was a very good year.
He led the River sales team...sang show tunes for fun,
He played walleyball, with Lindsay and all.
His muscles felt fine (mostly)
When he was 59.

And now he's 65, and it's a very good year.
He's kept his hundreds of friends like Kenny and Mark,
AJ, Harvey and Sym...
We're all thrilled to be here.
Steve's had a kick-ass career.
They've all been excellent years!

Jay Lufkin was the production director in the early River days. He was a pretty cool dude however, I'll never forget when he referred to my top money client as "Drunkin Donuts" and somehow a traffic/production order found its way to Dunkin's ad agency, Hill Holliday. I had to do some fancy footwork on that one.

Lisa Burgess was Steven's right-hand woman and worked with him for many years at the Bedford, NH office. I didn't see her often, but when I did we had some pretty good conversations. She had her pulse on everything that was happening in the company. Wish she could've worked out of the Haverhill office. Lisa is pretty cool in the most positive way.

So many stand-out people, so little time. The office staff whose duties ranged from traffic director to office manager included Julie Myers, Karen V, Stephanie Battagllia., Angela Rossi., Alaina, Jenna and Kim. Stephanie also did an air shift on Saturday mornings. All of the above were very kind and actually put up with me through the years. I would at times try to bribe them with cookies as well as ice cream deliveries. Sometimes that strategy worked!

I also need to mention Mark McKellar and Dennis Hennessey, two talented sales guys that I hired. Can't forget Bowtie Bill. That's Bill Phenix. Extremely intelligent and creative. Bill's role changed to National Sales Manager after I had left. Sources say, he excelled in that position. I'm very happy for him.

Kemp Dunn had come back for a second stint in sales at the River. Kemp is an accomplished drummer and plays with an incredible band called Grits & Groceries Orchestra. They were the winners of the 2016 Boston Blues Challenge and still perform today.

The list of co-workers that I looked forward to seeing every day is a long, long list. I know I'm running the risk here of leaving someone out. If I did, I'm sorry. I'm sure that we shared some special moments at 30 How Street. Allow me to mention a few more of my fellow salespeople. Jenni Dunn, Kristan Bishop, Pam Thompson, Lizzie Gorman, Bonnie Cartwright, Bethany Silva, Tracey Frye, Cindy G., Hannah, Veronica and the sports maven, Steve Accardi. First class co-workers that tried hard every day to win the battle on the streets. It was never easy but all of them had the right attitude and the personalities to make it work.

Then, there was the staple event of the River. The grand daddy of them all, the Newburyport Riverfront Music Festival in beautiful downtown Newburyport. It was a free concert, just like Woodstock. The big annual event would normally start at noon and run until dusk. Great River acts would perform on-stage to locals from Newburyport as well as P1 (radio term for our most avid listeners) River fans across New England. It was an annual tradition that would sometimes make the Newburyport Chamber of Commerce very nervous because of all those people converging on their town. What was amazing was that attendees would place their blankets and beach chairs in front of the stage the night before the concert! If you got there prior to the start of the event, you'd be hard-pressed to find any kind of space on the green grass.

The Revivalists rock Newburyport in 2016

Our premiere emcee, A.J. As Carly Simon sang, "nobody does it better!"

Lindsay holds up the guitar to be raffled off to one lucky spectator.

AJ announces the winner's name.

Unfortunately, I didn't win.

This wildly popular annual event made all of us at the River feel pretty cool. There was a ton of work to make it successful, but the team always seemed to pull it off with very little fanfare. Lindsay Burrill, our promotions director, was one of the key players when it came to making the event a winner. She certainly wasn't alone. Months of preparation that included solidifying the bands and the line-up, setting up the stage, selling sponsors who would sample products just outside of the concert venue and trying our best to make them happy, hiring extra policemen, working with the Newburyport Chamber, setting up a VIP party upstairs at the Firehouse Center of the Arts and even holding an indoor concert for our clients the night before the big event. I'm sure I left out a ton of details, but you get the point. The event moved a couple of years ago to Gloucester and is now referred to as the Seaside Music Festival.

Overall, my 14 years at the River was very positive. I didn't really like how my time ended there, but I know how proud I am of my accomplishments at a very special radio station. Steven Silberberg gave me the opportunity to grow as a sales manager, salesman and person, and I'll never forget him or the people I worked with.

Charlie, Kemp and me, before hitting the streets during a 'Survivor' sales promotion. We were soundly thrashed by the women!

Me as a blonde and the Halloween costume winner, Kim G.

Classic Billiards battle with Phenix, Finn+ Friedman.

Lizzy, Veronica and Jenni adding grace and style to the Riverfront Festival, Newburyport.

Marlene and Sarah, two of the nicest people you could ever work with.

Jackie on the right, she left me in the dust that day! Charity event to benefit the Emmaus Homeless Shelter

AJ, me and Matt at the River parking lot BBQ

Me and Trisch playing George and Martha Washington during a Presidents Day promotion

Team huddle prior to hoop action

Always good times at Cedardale

Promotions master Hisham from my early River days

The 3 Amigos

Annual Holiday Party at the River

CHAPTER ELEVEN

Valley 98.9, the Final Radio Station, Finally Benefits of Retirement

Pat Costa is a radio guy. He founded Costa Eagle Radio in 1995. We crossed paths through the years but I had never worked with him. He was a Merrimack Valley guy and owned and operated a beautiful facility in Methuen. His bread and butter was the Spanish language station, Power 102.9. Power was the top Spanish language radio broadcast in the Greater Boston area. Costa had acquired the WCCM signal and before I got there had hired my number two and three dads, Bruce Arnold and John Bassett. JB actually commuted from Milton on the South Shore to Methuen. That was quite a schlep, but JB still loved the social interaction and wasn't ready to call it a career.

Knowing that I was parting ways with the River, Pat and Deb Metros, his station's General Manager, reached out to me. There was a new radio station that was in its infancy stages called Valley 98.9. The format was primarily music of the 70's with a sprinkle of 60's and 80's in the mix. Lots of Billy Joel,

Elton John, Fleetwood Mac, Rod Stewart and the Eagles. On the air, you'd hear the slogan, "You know all the songs." Now, even though I was more of a 60's guy, I certainly knew all the songs from the 70's and was very comfortable selling air time to local business owners that were mostly baby boomers like me and had a soft spot for the music of that era.

Costa and Metros offered me the position as the station's General Sales Manager and I happily accepted. It was an interesting personal challenge for me to build sales revenue in the Merrimack Valley with a new radio station. In a way, my career came full circle and brought back my fond memories of selling air time for WCGY/WCCM. My sales staff primarily consisted of me and my good friend Dennis Finn. Dennis and I had worked together at the River and he was the driving force when it came to me joining him at Valley. I went to work weeding out my former River clients, those that would be appropriate on my newest radio station. That was a bit awkward since I had many friends still at the River, but when you go to a new radio station that's the first thing you do. You call your best client relationships and give them good reasons to give the new radio station a try. All is fair in love and war and there was certainly enough radio dollars to go around. I put together a sales plan for Pat and Deb and was off and running. My first thought was how we can further introduce the radio station to businesses in Southern New Hampshire. After all, the station's tower was located in Windham, NH, right across the Massachusetts border. I decided to design small bags with the station's logo and deliver the bags with candy to potential clients along busy Route 28 in Salem, NH. Not just any candy, but candy that was popular in the 1970's. Remember Candy Buttons, Twix, Charleston Chews, Reese's Pieces, Necco Wafers and Jelly Belly Jelly Beans? That's what I placed in the mini gift bags. I purchased the candy at the world's best candy store, Pearl's in Salem, NH. I felt that the candy idea would be a good introduction into the 70's theme of the radio station. The idea definitely opened some doors and resulted in a few sales. Pearl's is a supermarket of candy and I have to admit I bought a few items for my own sweet tooth including, are you ready for this? Chocolate-covered potato chips!!

Back to what was most important, SALES! Dennis and I made a pretty good team and in a short time grew our numbers and were well on our way to crushing our sales goals. Alex, Stephanie, Kevin and Julissa were a lot of fun to work with and helped me get accustomed to the way things operated at the station. As a bonus, I went back on the air after a 35 year hiatus. I wrote and voiced a weekly sports segment, sponsored by one of my favorite clients, Haffner's Oil and the likeable Joe Derry. Lots of positives, a few negatives, but after careful consideration and with mixed feelings I decided to call it a career and retire.

Me and Finn

The Benefits of Retirement

I often kid around and say, "Boy, this retirement thing is a lot of work!" Well it is, in a good way. You have to have a plan and simply do things that make you happy, like writing this book. You're also more conscious of taking care of your health by exercising and trying to eat better. With that said, I still have that never-ending sweet tooth and love my Mocha Chip ice cream from Richardson's, dark russet potato chips and blueberry crullers and donuts. Iced coffee from McDonald's is another one of my guilty pleasures. Now that this junk food talk has made me hungry, let's get back to the benefits of retirement.

1. You can get out of the bed when you want to

2. You have no daily rush hour traffic to contend with.

3. You get to set your own agenda.

4. You have fewer headaches because life is simpler.

5. You don't have to report to a boss about your actions.

6. You can put more time into creative pursuits.

7. You can go on vacations when you want to go and not when your employer says you can.

8. Every day is Saturday.

9. It's easier to be spontaneous.

10. You can take a nap when the urge hits.

11. Life is less predictable from 9 to 5.

12. You have the time to do all the things you always wanted but never had time for.

13. No more sales goals to worry about on a daily basis.

14. You could spend winters in Florida or hibernate in the comfort of your own home.

15. During the warmer months you could pick and choose what beach to visit and it doesn't have to be the weekends.

CHAPTER TWELVE

The Life of a Sports Geek

Yes, it's well documented by now. I'm a certified sports geek. Always have been and always will be. I was fortunate to spend seven years of my life as a sportscaster. Dreams certainly can come true. I covered the Celtics and Red Sox and had the opportunity to interview many of the prominent sports stars of the day. I have several stories on a few of them that are not fit to print in these pages. I was able to do play-by-play work for college and high school basketball and football, do daily sports reports, participate in a weekly sports talk show and now here I am writing about those fantastic adventures. In fact, even got the opportunity to step on the Fenway Park field and take ten swings at the Green Monster. Of course I didn't come close to hitting the ball over 315 feet, but it gave me chills to stand in the batting box where Yaz, Big Papi, Ted Williams, Freddy Lynn, Rico Petrocelli, and Dwight Evans stood. I hit a few ropes to right field but most of them trickled towards first and second base. It's a yearly event that the Red Sox offer their season ticket holders and one that I hope to continue when the event comes up again.

Want further proof of my sports 'geekness'? I have my own Sports Gallery in the basement of my home. There are over 500 pictures on the wall, including 27 sports collages that my dad contributed. In addition, I have one of Kevin McHale's size 17 sneakers, a huge Gronkowski cut-out, sports memorabilia, sports puzzles, autographed baseballs and a section dedicated to my dad, who was quite an athlete as well.

SPORTS SHORTS

One of my better sad sack stories happened at Randolph High while playing varsity basketball. I always made the team but my playing time was very limited. I sat on the bench and most likely led the league in splinters. My friends and family always came to cheer me on but they seldom had that chance. I would go onto the court for pre-game warm-ups, sit on the bench when the game started and return to the court at half-time to warm-up some more. My parents thought I looked pretty good during warm-ups and couldn't understand why I didn't play. Well one day it looked like that was about to change. There were two minutes left until half-time and Coach Carey called out my name. I was a bit nervous but at the same time couldn't wait to get on the court and strut my stuff. Then the coach told me what he wanted.

"Listen Yanofsky, Neil Schwartz (who happened to be our best player) just ripped his pants. At half-time I want you to change pants with him, got it?" Talking about bruising the ego of a 16 year old. So, taking one for the team, I went into the locker room and exchanged pants with Neil. At half-time I couldn't even take warm-up shots. I went directly to the bench with my legs closed, sat down and proceeded to root for my team and my pants. That was my junior year at Randolph High School. I quit the team during my senior year thinking that the coach was not a big fan of my basketball abilities. His loss!

Retiring from the R.H.S. basketball team I went on to play hoops for Randolph's U.S.Y. (United Synagogue Youth League). I was immediately inserted into the starting line-up by my new coach, Bob Gass. I was one of the team's top scorers, playing alongside such immortals like Steve Kaplan, Norm Wortzman, Mike Seidel, Joe Kovars, and Marc Golding. I really enjoyed playing U.S.Y. ball. The days of me leading the league in splinters were gone. My confidence made a comeback as well. *The Boston Globe's* Dan Shaughnessy had asked his readers to submit their best high school sports stories. I submitted the "shorts" story and Shaughnessy chose it as the best submission sent by his readers. He published it in his column the very next month. I wonder if Coach Cary ever saw the story.

THE 2013 BOSTON MARATHON

When I think of the word "tradition" the famous play *Fiddler on the Roof* pops into my head. "Tradition" was certainly one of the show's favorite tunes, basically performed by the entire ensemble. There's another tradition that has been on-going since 1897; the Boston Marathon, the world's oldest annual marathon event held 30 minutes away from my home.

The event is traditionally held on Patriots Day, the third Monday of April. That's when 30,000 runners start in Hopkinton and run through the streets and hills of Boston to the eventual finish line on Boylston Street, close to the Boston Public Library. Over 500,000 spectators cheer the runners on whether they know some of them or not. That brings me to my tradition. Every year for as long as I can remember, I'm one of those 500,000. I love the electricity of the day, the crowds clapping and encouraging the runners to keep going. I also admire the athletes who can run 26-miles. Now that's an accomplishment that I can't fathom.

When I think of my days on the track team at Randolph High School, I remember tiring at the end of a 220-yard race. Let me repeat that ridiculous distance again… 26 miles! Mercy!

On Marathon Day, most of the roads were blocked by 8:00am, so I would make sure I got there early that day to find a parking spot that would give me easy access and an escape when I decided to go home. Because I never can sit or stand still I do race day solo. It's my best day for exercise all year long as I normally walk about ten miles up and down the course from the finish line, up and down Boylston Street, Storrow Drive, Kenmore Square and Beacon Street. The early part of the day included the annual 11:00am Red Sox Patriots Day game at Fenway Park. I would go to the ballpark for the start of the game then leave around the fourth inning and head back to the marathon where the streets were filled with runners making their way to the finish line. Probably one of the most exhilarating moments in all of sports.

April 15, 2013 was going to be different. It was a cool but sunny comfortable day, perfect for the runners and the spectators. As I made my way towards the finish line, at the top of Boylston Street I ran into a friend, Sean McDonough. He was working at one of the bars alongside the marathon route adjacent to the fire station and across the street from the Hynes' Auditorium. We spoke for five minutes and then I was on my way. Equipped with my Canon for still pictures and a small video camera, I continued down Boylston snapping pictures when a pack of runners were about to pass by me. Sometimes the crowd was ten deep making it a challenge for me to get some good shots. I passed the Prudential Center and closed in on the finish line. The crowd was ecstatic, extremely vocal and enthusiastic. It was 2:50pm. I was now 25 yards from the finish line and decided to videotape some of the runners in their moment of glory. Then it happened; a deafening boom in front of me with smoke rising to the sky. It was an explosion that rocked Boylston Street and caused me to fall over another spectator. My first thought was that it was a bomb. Then just 12 seconds later in the other direction, a second explosion. At this point I was smack dab in the middle of this horrific war zone scene. People were virtually running for their lives in all different directions. I was shaken and scared and decided that I better get the heck out of there. I ran as fast as I could to Newbury Street where my car was parked, wondering if another bomb would explode at any moment. Along the way I was stopped by a mother and her two children. She asked me what had happened. I told her that two bombs went off near the finish line. She then gathered her children bringing them closer to her and asked me if they were safe. I told her to avoid Boylston Street and go home. Then, I was off like a bat out of hell trying to locate where I parked my car. I couldn't find it. As it turns out I ran past it by three blocks. Panic was quickly setting in and finally I found my car which for me at the time was my safe haven. Or was it? The first thing I did was put on the news station WBZ 1030 radio to see if there were more details of what just happened. I was surprised that they had nothing. Then I called my radio station 92.5 the River to hopefully go on the air and report what I had just seen. Karen Viens, our office manager, answered the phone. The conversation went like this.

Steve: Karen, I need to talk to Matt Phipps right away.

Karen: Steve, do you know that you're missing three pieces of copy? Where's the production order?

Steve: Karen, I'm at the Boston Marathon and two bombs just went off near the finish line. Get me Matt, I need to be on the air.

Karen: I'll try to find him, hold on, but don't forget about the production orders, you're way past the deadline.

Matt came to the phone and interviewed me along with Carolyn Morrell. I have to believe that I was the first person to report the events of the day on the radio. After all, it was only ten minutes after the bombings had occurred. From where I was sitting in my car I could see in the distance a portion of the marathon runners who were stopped by the police. Paula called me to see if I was okay. She knew I was at the marathon but not at the finish line.

The aftermath...

When something like this happens you tend to go over and over the details of what you just experienced. Here's my thoughts..

1. When I spoke with Sean on my way to the finish line for five minutes, I thought that if I were to talk to him for three minutes instead then I would've walked into the first bomb. If I spoke with him for seven minutes I most likely would've walked into the second bomb. The timing of the conversation most likely saved my life.

2. Prior to the explosions I walked up and down the right side of the road. This is the same side as the bombers who planted them. So, I must've passed by them maybe even two or three times.

3. Noting where I was when the bombs were detonated, I have to think that I was as close to the bombs as possible without getting hurt. Very, very lucky.

4. I didn't know it at the time, but four days later when I looked at what I captured on video I had more than I thought. It was a chilling video. First of people clapping, parents with their children in front of them in strollers, then the explosion caught on tape right in front of me.

5. The second part of the video captured me running down Newbury Street constantly repeating the words "oh my God, oh my God."

6. I never knew the camera was on all of this time and I even captured the mother with her children asking me what had happened. I was thoroughly discombobulated.

What happened as a result of the bombings? Three people had died. The first bomb took the life of a 29-year old woman; the second bomb killed a 23-year old woman and an 8-year old boy. Hundreds more were seriously injured and thousands more were scarred for life. The bombs were contained in pressure cookers hidden inside backpacks. The two bombers involved were 26 and 19 years old. I prefer not to acknowledge their names. A week or so passed and there was a memorial set up to honor the three that had perished. I needed to see the memorial. It was located right at the finish line of the marathon. It included their pictures and was draped with hundreds of flowers. There were many people there at the time paying their respects to the victims. I stood back from the crowd, leaning slightly against one of the brick buildings. A wave of emotion struck me and I had to fight back the tears. It was at that moment that a police officer approached me. I guess he had noticed that I was visibly upset. He asked me if I was all right. I told him that I was at the finish line that day and I felt extremely guilty that I ran away from the scene and didn't try to help those that were hurt. He told me that he was there as well and said, "You did the right thing. We were trying to clear all the spectators from the scene and had hundreds of qualified medical personnel to help those who needed it. After all, what would've you done if you saw someone with their limbs cut badly from the explosion?"

Well, he had a point there, but I still wish there was something I could've done. The cry of "Boston Strong" rang out throughout New England and beyond. I will never forget that day because of the lives lost, the dreams that were shattered and how two sick individuals could turn a wondrous day for 500,000 plus into a tragic day.

JACK THORNTON

My dream to someday work as a basketball announcer came to fruition in the early 80's. I covered two college teams, the St. Anselm Hawks and the New Hampshire College Penmen. I traveled with St. Anselm when the WKBR budget allowed me to do so. St. A's had just become a member of the Northeast-8. The eight conference teams that St. A's would be competing against included A.I.C., Assumption, Bentley, Bryant, Springfield, Stonehill and the University of Hartford. Other common opponents were NH College, Sacred Heart, Bridgeport, Merrimack and UMass Lowell. Occasionally we would play Division One schools. The two most notable mismatches were trips to Boston College and Harvard University. St. A's lost both games, they got destroyed by B.C. Future NBA star John Bagley played for B.C. at the time. The Hawks were handed a 56-point loss in that one. My good friend Marc Golding served as my color commentator and did an excellent job. St. A's made it very close against a huge Harvard team but fell short at the end by two points. I had a number of excellent color commentators. One was Ted Paulauskas, athletic director of St. A's. He reminded me of the knowledgeable Hubie Brown, former NBA coach and an insightful analyst.

The best color commentator, analyst or sidekick that joined me on the broadcasts was a fill-in for Ted Paulauskas. His name was Jack Thornton. Prior to the game, Ted told me that Jack was extremely good and that I'd enjoy working with him. Ted added, "Oh one more thing…..Jack is blind." When he said that I was taken aback but if Ted told me he was good, then he must be good. When I met Jack I found out very quickly that he was very knowledgeable about the players on both sides that were playing that particular night. As the game went on, I was in awe of Jack's ability to bring our listeners his own insight to what was happening on the basketball court. Plus, I was envious of his smooth delivery and his strong, professional sounding voice.

Following the game I asked Jack, "How do you do this and do it so well?" He told me that based on listening to the inflection of my voice, the sound of the dribbling of the basketball, as well as the enthusiasm or the lack of enthusiasm from the crowd, he would generate his thoughts and translate it into his quick and sometimes witty commentary. I spoke with Ted Paulauskas recently and he told me that back in the 80's when he coached St. A's, Jack would sit on the bench during practices. Ted would ask Jack his opinion on the defensive scheme that was being taught to his players. Ted added, "He was always spot on!" Yes, Jack was the best analyst that I ever worked with. Or should I say the incredible Jack Thornton.

REMEMBERING MY FIRST GAME AT FENWAY

It was 1963. I was 10 years old. My dad brought me to my first Red Sox game at Fenway Park. When we entered the ballpark I was in awe of the park, especially the green, green grass that seemed to go on forever leading to the left field wall and around to right field and the bleachers. This was a truly magical moment in my life. Finally, I was going to see a baseball game and the players I emulated in my driveway 'live' and in living color! We went early to watch the Red Sox take batting practice. My dad and I walked right down to the first row. Within minutes, a very tall Red Sox pitcher came over to greet the fans. His name was Gene Conley. He was a giant. I never saw anyone that stood 6' 10" tall. Conley was a rare athlete who also played basketball for the Boston Celtics. My breath was taken away as the gentle giant approached my father and I and said, "Hey kid, catch this." He proceeded to take the baseball and in Bob Cousy-like fashion flipped the ball to me from behind his back! OMG, this was a defining moment in my life in which I became a HUGE Boston Red Sox fan. I guess you could say that it was that baseball season that I also learned to hate the dreaded New York Yankees. Roger Maris, Mickey Mantle, Tom Tresh, Whitey Ford, Moose Skowron and Tony Kubek were just a few names that made my skin crawl, even at 10 years old. The Yankees were the toughest team to beat in baseball, but somehow, some way and someday we would beat those guys.

A SECRET UNDERCOVER MISSION

The old Boston Garden or as we say it around here, "Gahden" opened its doors for the first time in 1928. My father was four years old. It was called Boston Madison Square Garden, the Boston version of New York's Madison Square Garden. Shortly thereafter, it was changed to simply the Boston Garden.

History tells us that the Boston Celtics began their inaugural season at the Garden in 1946. We also know that outside of sporting events, the Garden hosted many concerts including Elvis, the Beatles and the Jackson Five. Another interesting tidbit of Garden lore is that JFK in November of 1960 held a political rally in front of a massive crowd of 22,000. I didn't know that the Garden could ever hold that amount. I remember the number that the Celtics would always use in referring to a sell-out crowd and it was 13,909. I suppose that with no basketball court or hockey rink, that amount of people could be accommodated. Obviously, JFK packed them in like sardines!

I actually attended a sales seminar in the building by motivational speaker Tom Hopkins. Well, all good things must come to an end. In 1998, the Boston Garden was demolished. There were several issues including broken seats, structural issues and sanitary problems. The last event in the building happened in 1995 when the Bruins played the New Jersey Devils in the NHL Playoffs. The Fleet Center replaced the Boston Garden and opened its doors for the first time in September of 1995.

A few months earlier on April 21, I actually attended the last Celtics game in the fabled old building. That game was a Celtics' defeat at the hands of the New York Knicks. While at the game, I remember a loud banging sound about 25 rows up from my section. When I turned around I saw a gentleman (and I use the term loosely) with a hammer and screwdriver in hand, trying his best to pull out one or multiple seats for his own personal collection. He had just lifted a seat out of the row when two policemen approached and arrested him. It was an idiotic thing to do, but I guess you can't blame a guy for trying.

Now let's return to the title of this segment, A Secret Undercover Mission. There was lots of news coverage regarding the opening of the new Garden. Private tours were granted to big businesses throughout the city. At the time, I was working with Joe DiDonato at WSSH. Joe and I read about the private tours that would be passing through the new building. On that day, Joe said, "Let's go down there and see if we can get in." Well, if my boss tells me to do something, I normally jump. In addition, this was a work day and we'd have to sneak out with no one in the office noticing. Maybe this is one of the reasons that I was so fond of Joe! So here we are entering the new building. We looked as if we belonged there with our $300 suits, (slight exaggeration) shiny polished shoes and our impressive Burberrys of London stylish ties. As we scoped out the lay-out to determine how to infiltrate one of the many tours that were currently in progress, it was obvious that we had to make our way into an elevator that would take us to the next level. There were several police officers standing around, possibly looking for people like Joe and I. We continued to walk right towards the main elevator where we were greeted by a security guard. He didn't say a word as we entered the elevator filled with businessmen. The elevator door closed and we were on our way to the main floor where the tours were being held. Of course, we didn't know what was waiting for us at the time. It's called living on the edge. As we left the elevator, our next obstacle was about 20 yards in front of us. It was a long table manned by new Garden staffers. At each table, there were hundreds of name tags. Maybe this was where our journey would end…..or maybe not. Joe and I were greeted by the staff members as we approached the table. This particular table was a mixture of employees' name tags from either Merrill Lynch or Fidelity. I went to the right, Joe went to the left and simultaneously we chose one of the name tags as our own. I remember saying, "Oh, there I am," and then picked up the tag of the name that I would assume was reserved for the tour and headed to the entrance of the new Garden with Joe right behind me. We looked inside and saw this magnificent looking structure. Two minutes later we were approached by one of the Garden employees. They looked at our name tag with the company's name prominently displayed and told us that our group's tour would be starting in a few minutes. She then started to lead us to the rest of our supposed co-workers. Well, we had seen enough and politely said to the woman, "Thanks very much, but we must return to the office." We know we couldn't be seen with our false name tags and possibly be revealed as the imposters that we were. Joe and I escaped and our own personal tour was complete!

REFLECTIONS OF A CHAMPIONSHIP

It was 2008 and the Boston Celtics had just walloped the LA Lakers 131-92 to win their first NBA championship in 22 years. My wife and son called me crazy when I felt compelled to get in my car at midnight, on a work night and drive to the Boston Garden to join thousands of crazed fans to celebrate the victory. Parking at Faneuil Hall, I headed to the Garden. It took me about five minutes to realize that my wife and son were probably right. I never made it to the Garden as hundreds of police officers with shields on their faces and looking like something out of a *Star Wars* movie were pushing the crowd back. As I encountered some unruly punks knocking over newspaper stands, toppling barrels and destroying street signs, I came to the conclusion that this wasn't anywhere close to the celebration I was expecting. I was witnessing a drunken display of idiocy. With an army of policeman heading towards me I quickly retreated and ran for my life! Definitely time to head home. I waited in the parking lot until 2:00am. No one was moving. The lot was packed with people in their vehicles honking their horn and shouting out obscenities. Finally, I made some headway, escaped the maddening crowd and got home slightly after 3:00am. It certainly wasn't one of my prouder moments.

The next opportunity to celebrate the Celtics championship was to attend the Celtics parade in Boston. There were thousands and thousands of people. It was insane, but certainly non-violent and a lot more fun. The best moment for me was getting a close-up look at Paul Pierce on the Duck Boat, puffing away on a cigar, obviously a tribute to Red Auerbach. He was grinning from ear-to-ear. It was a joyous event and since basketball is my favorite sport, I knew that I had to be there. Prior to the parade, I remember reading an article by LA sports columnist TJ Simers, summarizing the series. I'm paraphrasing:

"The Lakers are an embarrassment. They went to the NBA finals, the Celtics suffering injuries to several starters along the way and still couldn't measure up. The difference between the champs and the chumps was striking. Make all the excuses you want and the Laker fans will, but the guys in purple lacked the competitive drive that the Celtics exhibited from start to finish in this series. Some athletes live for opportunities like this, but several key performers for your beloved Lakers wilted when the going got tough. Two teams go for the title and one of them has to lose, but that doesn't mean getting pulverized and exposed as big softies---the Lakers laying down like whipped dogs. Laker fans will spend the next few days offering excuses, rebuttals and sharp retorts while trying to ignore the obvious—their heroes lack the heart and true grit to be champs." And then from a Laker fan who wrote in the LA Times...."After watching the Lakers-Celtics series, I think the wrong coach is getting the $10 million a year." (Phil Jackson had that kind of contract and Doc Rivers did not)

For me, my favorite Celtic that season had to be Kevin Garnett. The guy is a nut, but in the good sense of the word. What's a step above being passionate? He set the tone and the attitude for the entire season and didn't let up. Raising banner number 17 to the Boston Garden rafters was a great moment in their long storied franchise history. To say that this was a good time to be a Boston sports fan is a huge understatement. Congratulations to the Boston Celtics!! You certainly made me smile.

MOSES REVIEWS THE EAST COAST BASEBALL DRAFT

Since one of my passions is writing about sports, I have always appointed myself as the league scribe when it comes to the many fantasy/rotisserie leagues that I've joined through the years. Not sure if everyone in the league reads them but hopefully some do and just maybe it puts a smile on their faces. For those of you unfamiliar with fantasy/rotisserie leagues, here's a short explanation. A group of friends, normally 10-12, get together prior to the season and take turns drafting players from the major league teams. In this example, the East Coast Baseball League, each of us draft players from either the

American or National League. When our roster has been completed we're all ready for the start of the season. Based on how our players perform we are awarded points in the standings for multiple categories such as batting average, home runs, pitcher strikeouts, wins, etc. There's a lot more to it, but it's certainly a blast watching a baseball game and rooting for your players to do well. After all, you could win a few dollars at the end of the season and from a competitive standpoint finish ahead of your buddies. I'm a bit obsessed with these leagues but for the most part it's not so bad. I also participate in basketball and football leagues.

Thought I'd include a sample of my work written for the East Coast baseball league a few years back. I don't think that you have to be a baseball aficionado to appreciate it, maybe just a fan of Moses.

Time for my round three re-cap. I wanted to get a guest writer for this segment. I limited down to four candidates. Guerin Austin, Bob Ryan, Don

Rickles, and finally, Moses. As I celebrate Passover, Moses was the overwhelming choice. Passover, of course is a Jewish holiday that lasts for eight days to commemorate the freedom of the Israelites from the Egyptians. In the Torah, God helped the people of Israel escape with the leadership of Moses by casting 10 plagues on the Egyptians so that he would release the Jews from his reign of terror. How does Passover relate to our draft and fantasy baseball?

PASSOVER, when it comes to drafting our respective teams refers to the players that we Passed-Over and the curious selections that we came up with. Moses is a very wise man and it's little known that he was a huge Angels fan. Obviously throughout his illustrious career, he was aided by angels. Later on in his life, his favorite movie was *Angels in the Outfield.* If Moses were alive today, no doubt he would've made a great defensive lineman or even a professional wrestler.

Charlton Heston, who played Moses in *The Ten Commandments,* had muscles upon muscles. In the movie version, Heston defeated Yul Brynner who played the Pharaoh of Egypt rather handily. In fact if you were keeping score, it was a four game sweep. The final game when Moses miraculously parted the Red Sea was almost rained out. But after a two-hour delay, the game was now completed. Perhaps Moses' wooden staff might have suited him well as a baseball bat. My guess is that he wouldn't miss many outside pitches and that his launch angle would be record-breaking. The children of Israel said "Who shall go up for us first?" (Judges 20:18)

Moses was a man of few words, but when he spoke, his words and wisdom counted. Moses put down his wooden staff to write about the third round in the East Coast baseball league.

Pick #1 in Round 3: NINJA's

Oy vey, Trevor Bauer? I think that David (of Goliath fame) could throw the ball or a sling shot better than the unstable Mr. Bauer. If I could once again talk to the BIG GUY and he allowed me to add another commandment, it would be, "Thou shalt not throw the ball over the centerfield fence just because you gave up four runs in one inning." May be tough to fit on the tablet, but who does this guy think he is? Then, I looked at your list of pitchers. Double Oy-Vey. What a pitiful list. Carrasco, Heaney, Stroman, Archer, Price and Kluber. That's a sad lot. In case you missed it, this clown Bauer also sliced his finger with a drone. He's a certified nutcase. Good luck to Brian with this heavenly or maybe more appropriately, hellish selection.

Pick #2 in Round 3: LOOSE CLEATS

The Cleats selected Eugenio Suarez. This power hitting machine was recently diagnosed with a sore shoulder. I can relate to that. As I climbed down Mt. Sinai with the 10 Commandments, the tablets did a number on my shoulders. To add insult to injury, I had to walk in the desert for another 40 years. That didn't help me either. On the positive side, this guy Suarez hit 49 bombs last season. Holy Moses! 600-plus plate appearances over each of the past four seasons. Home run totals go up and up each year. Sore shoulder? Give him two Tylenol and call me in the morning. Why wasn't Tylenol invented during my long walks in the dessert. Bad timing I guess. Good selection by Toby.

Seventh inning stretch trivia…

Question: What happened during the first baseball game in the Bible?

Answer: Eve stole first, Adam stole second, Cain struck out Abel and then the Giants and the Angels were rained out.

Pick #3 in Round 3: The Lyfters Tommy Edman was Alan's choice. I'll have to check my scrolls to confirm. Edman may be one of the chosen people but in this case, the Lyfters chose him way too soon. *Heavenly Illustrated*, the bible of fantasy sports news had him ranked as the 462nd player. True, he's only 24 years young but I would've taken a deep breath and passed on him. When I was that age, I was checking out the Red Sea and the possibility of parting it in the near future. I knew that I was going to need a lot of help, but as you know it all worked out well in the end. There were 20 or more higher ranked second basemen at the time. Who knows? Maybe another miracle?

Since 1998, I've really enjoyed competing in fantasy baseball leagues against some pretty good friends. As you can see from the previous page, I also get a kick out of writing. The leagues are very competitive and if you know me at all then you know that I love to compete. The commissioner of the East Coast Baseball League is Guy Dickinson. Guy spends a tremendous amount of time inputting the league, the daily transactions, creating the rules and more. I appreciate all his hard work to keep the league going for over two decades.

The Executive Baseball League is led by Mitch Fishman, who also does a phenomenal job running the league. Mitch is also one of my poker buddies. Then, there's the Executive Basketball League led by Brian Feigenbaum. Another noteworthy league member that I'd like to mention is George Kayes, a retired police officer. George and I have participated in many of the same leagues. He's a guru when it comes to sports knowledge and even takes trips with his better half Marie down to Florida to do a little scouting at spring training games and of course to soak up the sun. Paula and I connected with George and Marie in Florida. I always wanted to attend a spring training game or two in the Sunshine State and joined George and Marie for the games and some sunny beach time.

I spend a ton of time participating in these leagues and doing research, hoping to get an edge on the competition. I would have to say that overall the leagues are 60% luck and 40% skill. Injuries to key players can really bring a team down and destroy your chances to finish "in the money"

Somehow my wife puts up with all of those games and even has to listen to me complain about my underachieving players. Thank goodness she's a sports fan.

By the way, the name of all of my teams regardless of the sport has been the Y's Guys. Probably an appropriate name.

I was very fortunate to have met some of the athletes that I admire. Sometimes it was in the locker room when I was a sportscaster, other times it was meeting them at the ballpark or the arena. Here are a few of those 'geeky' sports memories.

K.C. Jones and Curt Gowdy at a Lowell car dealership, one of my clients at the time

Me and the Chief, Robert Parish, at a Celtics practice

Wade Boggs at the 1986 World Series

Luis Tiant at Fenway

Mr. Everything, Bob Ryan

The late great John Havlicek

CHAPTER THIRTEEN

Pieces of Poetry, Randomly Speaking

BRADY AT THE SNAP

(My attempt at sports poetry, with apologies to Ernest Lawrence Thayer, author of *Casey at the Bat*)

The outlook wasn't brilliant for the Patriots eleven that day;
The score stood nine to three, the Giants led, yet there were still three quarters left to play.

But the Pats marched down the field, Brady took control of the game… and all of New England rejoiced; Knowing that this Superbowl result would not be the same.

Touchdown! Brady found Woodhead, all smiles as he passed the goal line;
And so at halftime the score in favor of the Pats was ten to nine.

The halftime show featured Madonna as she pranced across the stage;
While inside the locker room, the players had to listen to their respective coaches' rage.

The third quarter began, the Pats had the ball and Brady connected for ten passes in a row;
The first one, a shocker complete to Ochocinco!

Down the field they went, then a 12-yard touchdown to Hernandez came with 3:40 left on the clock;
The score now 17-9 and the Pats looked to be a surefire lock.

Suddenly the Giants stormed back, adding two field goals to the score;
The Pats had their chances but couldn't figure out how to close the door.

Then the moment came when all Patriots fans yelled 'damn.'
It was a 38-yard pass play from Manning to Manningham.

How did he catch the ball? What the heck?
And to add insult to the play, he caught it right in front of coach Belichick.

Bradshaw ended the 88-yard drive with a touchdown of his own;
57 seconds left for Brady to overcome the lead that his team had blown…

There was ease in Brady's manner as he stepped into the snap,
There was pride in Brady's bearing as Gisele held their son in her lap.

To win the big game, the G-men just needed a few stops;
The Pats receivers said OK and obliged with some terrible key drops.

Now it was down to the last play, a Hail Mary was in store;
Brady cranked his arm and towards the end zone the ball would soar…

A traffic jam of players were gathered all around;
Gronk was the closest, but could he catch it or would the ball find the ground?

Thousands watching at the game and millions watching on TV;
They could only hold their breath; the final score was seconds away to see.

Oh somewhere in this favored land the sun is shining bright, the band is playing somewhere and somewhere hearts are light.

And we know that someday, Brady and his coach will be elected to the Football Hall of Fame;
But on this day, whether you like it or not, the hated Giants won the game.

Did it really matter that we lost that one? More Super Bowl championships to come.   We're so spoiled, don't you think?

TWAS THE NIGHT BEFORE PASSOVER

Twas the night before Passover, when all through the night;
The brisket was still settling and the brownies were a pleasant sight.

Paula, who had prepared for the feast was all nestled in bed;
While the perfect Passover Sedar danced in her head.

All of a sudden there arose such a clatter;
She whacked her husband Steve to see what was the mater.

What the heck he said as he was comfortably restin;
When he peaked out the window, there was a guy that looked like Moses or maybe even Charlton Heston!

Were they having a Passover dream as they watched this bearded old man moving quite slow;
After all, the story happened three thousand years ago.

Paula and Steve pondered opening the door, wondering if they should risk it;
It was really Moses and he said that all the way from the Holy land, he could smell Paula's brisket.

He didn't say much as he held up his staff;
And as he pointed to the refrigerator, the stunned couple let out a nervous laugh.

We were in awe of his presence and overall he seemed fine;
Upon further review, Moses only stopped by for some Manischewitz wine.

After his long journey he guzzled the bottle, thanked us and said his good-byes;
This man with the staff represented the joyous holiday of Passover and all that was wise.

We just couldn't understand why he didn't ask for some brisket, not even a bite;
As he mounted his donkey, he looked at us and said Happy Passover to all and to all a good night.

SNOW

It's quiet and peaceful, Belknap Drive is dressed in white;
With four layers of clothing and two feet of snow, I'm just hoping that the snow is light.

I stop for awhile catching my breath and begin to ponder life;
Wondering why I'm out here and inside, nice and warm is my wonderful wife.

It's cold, the snow is actually heavy, so I have to ask you this;
If we didn't have winter, what would we really miss?

OK, skiers, down the slopes you must fly;
Never understood that and have no desire to try.

So those that love the snow you can call me a wimp;
I'd prefer that instead of dressing up and looking like the Goodyear blimp.

And oh, then there's the idiots who love to speed in the snow;

While I stay in the right lane, blinkers on, going frightfully slow.

Can't even drive in the streets with the white walls blocking your view;
Slowly inching out to the road, not really knowing what to do.

So for me, the snow and the winter just gives me more stress;
Whether walking in it, shoveling or driving, it's just one big mess.

Maybe now you see my point of view and with me you might go;
To Hawaii, Florida or the west coast to San Diego.

So give me the shovel, I'll finish the snow job and clear the walkway;
Back to reality, it's here in New England, I'll probably stay.

A DAY TO REMEMBER

This will be a day to remember,
A day mom and dad will never forget.

The greatest day of them all;
When Mom and Dad and baby first met.

Welcome to this world, you're truly a dream come true;
Everything you do will be a first, everything you do will be brand new.

So many wondrous things to look forward to, some big and some small;
There's hugs and kisses, riding a bike, eating ice cream and even watching the Patriots play football.

There will be some sad times, but many more happy times, that's for sure;
Every day an adventure, every day you'll grow and learn a lot more.

You'll learn that there's nothing like a sunny day when you have absolutely nothing to do;
You'll smile, laugh and cry and wonder why the ocean and sky shine a brilliant blue.

But the one thing you should learn that's more important than the rest;
Is to take the time to learn to love and then you'll pass the test.

Understand that people have feelings and deep down inside we're really all the same;
But treating people the way you'd like to be treated is such an important part of the game.

With parents who already love you, I can tell you're off to a great start;
So my final piece of advice to you is to love and cherish every day and always listen to your heart.

LIFE IN HEAVEN, A TRIBUTE TO MY DAD… May 2012

It was Lou's first full day in Heaven and there was so much to do.
The welcoming committee was led by Brass, Whitman, Rutman and the rest of the Lucerne Street crew.

Then all of a sudden, out of nowhere, a golden limo appeared and angels began to sing;
Out stepped the driver and of course the driver was the one and only Bing.

They hugged and kissed, as Lou's older brother told him how much he had been missed.

Out from the limo an overpowering presence appeared for all to see;
Yes it was the man himself and on his Calvin Klein jacket was the sparkling letter "G"

The lord welcomed Lou and offered him one special request;
Lou thought for a moment and in no time came up with what he thought would be the best.

There was ease in the Lord's manner and so much comfort in his voice;
Then Lou spoke up and said, 'If you could restore my leg, that would be my first choice.

No problem said the Lord, consider it done;

In a flash his leg was restored and then the welcome party begun

Pennies from Heaven by Bing was the opening song;
Lou was digging the tunes, but he knew he couldn't stay long.

After all, it was his first 'Mother's day in heaven, so he picked up his I-phone and called his mother; And then who appeared right in front of his eyes, it was Marshall, his younger brother.

He spoke with his mother Rose and his father Joe who he hadn't seen in years;
At that moment, it was difficult for Lou to hold back his tears.

Lloyd stopped by and welcomed him with a Rob Roy;
Lou looked at him and beautiful memories came back, when Lloyd was a young handsome boy.

Everett made an appearance with Nanny in a vehicle that he had created;
And according to Heaven News, his invention was very highly rated.

So, Lou's big party was in the works to welcome him back;
The guest list included J.F.K., Cassius Clay, Marilyn Monroe and all his favorites known as the Rat Pack.

Lou thought for a moment and knew that back on earth there would be lots and lots of tears;
But one more time he wanted to remind us that he had 87 incredible years.

CHAPTER FOURTEEN
Picture My Family

Ma and Dad strut their stuff on the dance floor

Ready for my first date.

Family dining

Dad and his two boys

Ma and her two boys.

Dad, Kenny, Bing, Marshall and me.

Kenny, Nanny and a bearded guy

Nanny and Everett

The six of us.

Cruising on the Odyssey.

These crazy kids were married for 61 and a half years!!!

What a salesman! I sold Paula on the idea of marrying me! 2021 marks our 40st anniversary!

Our wedding song was "Here, There and Everywhere" by the Beatles

I think we were on our way to Kelly's Roast Beef.

Provincetown, as a huge fish hovered behind us.

In the Red Sox dugout. We threw the players out or maybe it was an off day and we never saw any players. You can decide.

We're in a New York state of mind.

How did I get gray and Paula stays the same?

My fantastic in-laws, Bernie and Bernice! Loving, caring and generous. They loved their winters in Jupiter, Florida. I thought it was pretty cool that they had towels made that had their initials, B.E + B.E. As long as I took care of their daughter, all was well in the world.

Bernice and Bernie

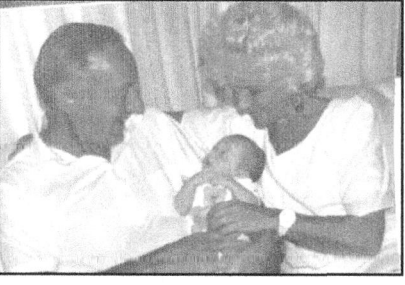

1988, a very special year. Hello, Daniel, Love at first sight.

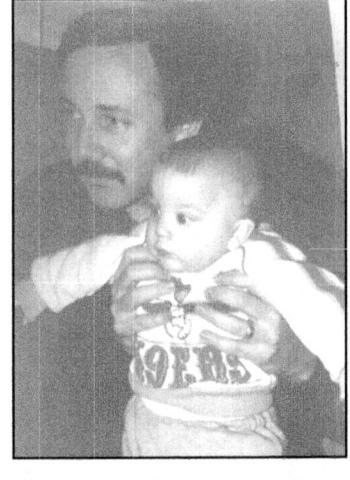

49ers outfit, What's up with that?

Some of my favorite pictures.

200

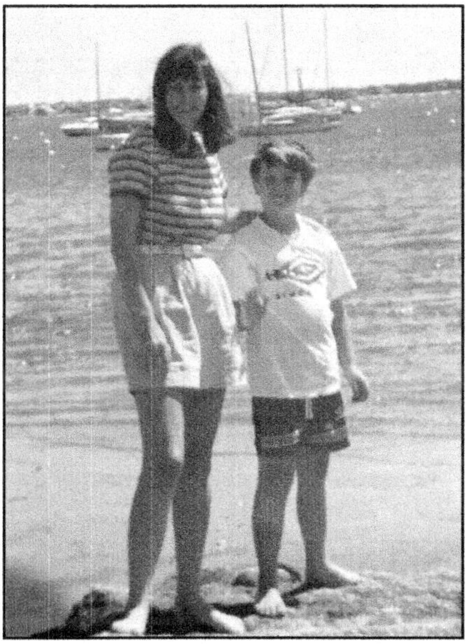

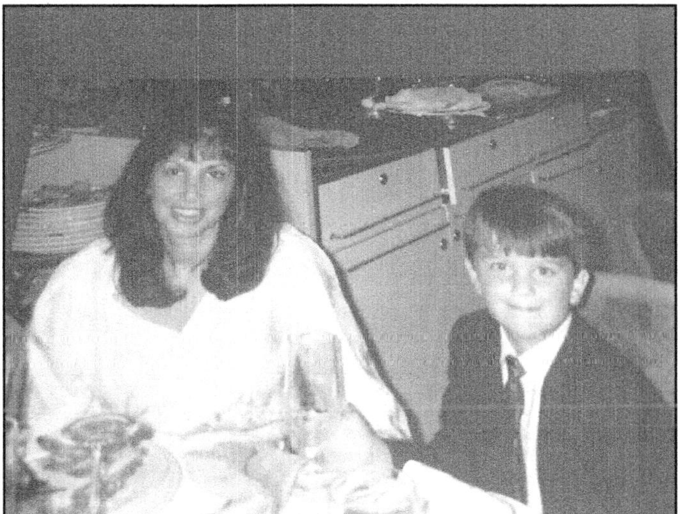

You could tell at an early age we had a drummer in the family.

My all-time favorite pic of Daniel

Family gathers in Andover.

The greatest game!

My incredible Aunt Carole

Nantasket Beach, Hull.

Brothers on the open sea.

Rachel and Daniel sharing some quality time.

A tux? Must be Riverfest.

Rhonda, Elaine, Me, Kenny and Mike.

Rachel, Daniel and Stacy.

Loving Grandmothers.

The famous Carnegie Deli in NY, now that's what I call a sandwich! Love those steak fries, too!

Enjoying Passover with the Davidson's and Ruthie.

Fenway Pa-hk.

28-3, sound familiar?

My two favorite people in the world

CHAPTER FIFTEEN

Dad's Behind the Eight Ball

From the pool halls in Dorchester to my pool table in Andover, dad always excelled at billiards. He tried to teach me "positioning" or setting yourself up for your next shot. Dad explained that the best way to learn "positioning" was by playing the game nine-ball. His advice on billiards was as savvy as his advice was on playing poker. He was quite good at that game as well and played weekly with his buddies. They'd play high stakes poker for 10 cents to 25 cents a hand. Normally he'd win. He would also keep track of his wins and losses. Gee, I wonder who I got that tracking system from?

One New Year's Eve we had a billiards tournament with Daniel and some friends and of course, dad wanted to join in. Probably to show all us whipper-snappers how the game is played. Now keep in mind, Lou Yanofsky was in his mid-80's but had us all by 20

years or so in experience. We played until the clock struck midnight and the results may not surprise you. They surprised me. Dad was the best pool player all night long. It was an impressive display, one that would put a smile on the face of Minnesota Fats.

A few months later, Dad came over and once again challenged me to a best-of-seven match. We were tied three games apiece, so it went down to game seven to determine who would be the King of the Hill, A-number-1 and, of course, top of the heap. After missing an easy shot, Dad complained, "Oh my eyesight is terrible, I can't see a thing." At that moment I realized that I couldn't win no matter what I did. If I did win, then I'd be beating up on an 85-year old that could barely see. If I lost, then I would've been beaten by a guy who could barely see. Well, the seventh game was now official and in the books. Dad won four games to three. *This photo was his idea and the beers haven't been touched in 20 years.*

Abe and Louie's, best steakhouse in Boston

Disney Dad

CHAPTER SIXTEEN

Merry and Daniel and a Couple of Cool Cats

We have been blessed with an incredible son, Daniel and his wonderful wife, Merry, short for Meredith. Since I've written this book in 2021, this coming October, they'll be celebrating their fifth year anniversary. *Mazel Tov!* Maybe I'm a little biased but their wedding held at the Villa in East Bridgewater was the best wedding ever, even if my speech to the newlyweds lasted a little over an hour. (just kidding, but as always I did have a lot to say) After all, we have only one son and I really needed to make this one count.

Richard Davidson walks Merry down the aisle

I now pronounce you man and wife! Childhood friend Matthew presides over the ceremony.

Let's get this party started!

OK, if we must. Time for two speeches from the dads.

Two extremely proud mothers.

It's a wrap…Congratulations!

Aww, my baby's no longer a baby!

Men, Men, Men, Men……manly men.

Joyce, Harvey and Gail enjoying the festivities.

WITH TWO CATS IN THE YARD

Graham Nash once sang the popular song "Our House" and its lyrics; "With two cats in the yard, life used to be so hard, now everything is easy cause of you."

Well, Luna and Oatmeal do not spend much time in the yard, but they've certainly been a welcomed addition to the Yanofsky household.

Luna, on the left is the older sister and it seems here that Oatmeal looks up to her. Loveable cats who are also very good at playing hide and go seek.

Luna and her customized pillow

Oatmeal poses upside down

TRAVEL AGENTS EXTRAORDINAIRE

OK, I admit it. I'm always kvelling (bursting with pride or satisfaction for those of you not familiar with the word) over my son and his bride. Daniel is the General Manager of a very successful café in Beverly, along with being a talented drummer, an expert on food, a movie trivia guru, very handy around the house, but most importantly a great son, husband and a thoughtful friend. Merry is pretty wonderful as well too. She's a special needs teacher in the Andover School system, a devoted friend, kind and loving. Yet, they're able to balance it all and still find the time to serve as our official travel agents.

Over the past several years, they have organized our trips and they normally center on their passion, which is running. We're more than fine with that because we get to see different parts of the country, watching them run 5K races, half-marathons and even the big daddy of them all, a full 26.2 mile event. One of our favorite trips took place in the beautiful city of Savannah, Georgia. It was here that Merry and Daniel ran the Rock N' Roll Marathon.

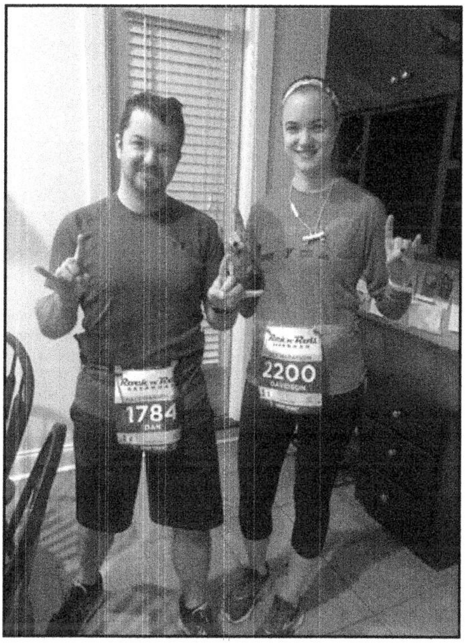
1784
2200

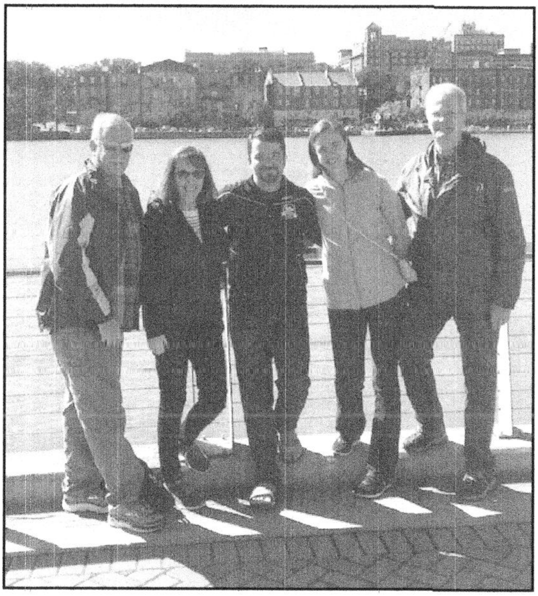

I don't trust the guy in the middle.

Richard D., a very worthy travel companion

It was Merry and Daniel's first full marathon and we were all very lucky that it took place at Disneyworld in Orlando, Florida. True, the temperatures were in the 80's, not so lucky for all the runners, especially those that were running their first 26-mile event. The trip included Merry's parents, Linda and Richard. Let me take a moment here to mention something about these two very special people (this might be the 20th time I've used the word 'special,' I'll have to go back and count). When someone marries into a family, you've sort of inherited the new relatives that come along with the new union. In this case, boy did we luck out.

I really don't know many families whose sons or daughters got married and both sets of parents became close. In fact, none come to mind. Linda and Richard Davidson are special, caring and thoughtful people. We have shared holidays, family gatherings, BBQ's and at the top of the list, vacation trips to cheer our children on and support their passion for running and the accomplishments that come with it.

A Special Disney vacation.

They both finished the marathon.

As Richard watched all the action.

Merry and Daniel run everywhere and in all kinds of weather.

We've been very lucky to travel around the country with Merry and Daniel. There was, however, one trip that stands out to me. That was our four hour ride to the Baseball Hall of Fame in Cooperstown, New York. We then continued the journey north for another four hour ride to Niagara

Falls. (Slowly I turn, step-by-step....Every time I hear Niagara Falls, I can't help thinking of the Three Stooges)

I was on the mound that day, Daniel as my battery mate. Ruth struck out on three pitches.

CHAPTER SEVENTEEN

Jacqui, Jacqueline, Jackie and Ma

Yes, all of the four above names are rolled up into one pretty special (there's that word again) person, my mother. As I write this book, Ma is a spritely 90-years young. She has adjusted quite well since my father's death in 2012. Of course, she often tells me that she misses him more now than ever. But, after selling her home in Randolph and moving twice since then, she's been extremely resilient. One amazing fact about Jacqui is that at 90 she takes no medications whatsoever and is still able to walk without the benefit of a cane.

Ma doing a yard sale at 16 Clark Street.

Jacqueline continues to watch her favorite TV shows, *Friends, Gilmore Girls* and the *Golden Girls*. Of course, I'd be remiss if I didn't mention her love of the Boston Red Sox. This love affair with the team didn't happen until around the year 2010. One night during a late Red Sox game on TV, she called me at midnight. When the phone rang and seeing it was her, I was terrified to pick up the phone. I said, "Ma, what's the matter, are you all right?" She said, "Can you believe that Farrell (Red Sox manager at the time) left that pitcher in so long?" I said, "Ma, I love to talk baseball with you, but please don't call me at midnight unless there's an emergency, OK? You really did scare me." Ma's favorite players through the years have been Jacoby Ellsbury and then Andrew Benintendi. Reliable sources tell me that those two players were the cutest on the team.

We helped my mother sell our Randolph house in 2020. She had been there for 56 years. Needless to say, it held a ton of memories. Since then she moved into an apartment in Newton and then to the Shillman House in Framingham, a wonderful community that she really enjoys. Her long time friend Cynthia Silverstein has lived there for awhile and was very excited when she learned that Ma would be joining her. Ma has always boasted to her family that when she was nine months old, she won a contest for being the healthiest baby. I'll take her word for it.

A nice day at the old ballpark

Ma hits the big 9-0 in a wild celebration in Andover!

CHAPTER EIGHTEEN

Good Friends Are Hard to Find,
Unless You Met Them in High School

Here's a corny yet appropriate Irish saying…

"There are good ships and wood ships, ships that sail the sea, but the best ships are friendships and may they always be!"

I graduated Randolph High School in 1971. That means that at the time of writing this book, it's been a half of a century since I received my diploma. Because of the pandemic, there is no immediate plans for a 50- year reunion. It's certainly hard to believe that I could possibly be that old. I guess it should be expected when you're born in 1953. With that said, here's something that you don't see or hear about every day.

My closest friends today are my high school friends of 1971. Even though we're spread out from the South Shore to the North Shore of Massachusetts, and all the way to Omaha, Nebraska, we're all still pretty close. I'm sure that many people stay in touch with one or two high school friends, but I'm talking about many more. We've shared life's ups and downs for five decades. In addition, we've gone on trips to Las Vegas and to Florida and celebrated many happy times at the weddings of our children. Keeping in touch is not always easy. After all, we have our own lives that keep us busy. But as the above saying states so clearly. "Good friends are like stars, you don't always see them, but you know they're always there." I've stayed close to several of my "radio family" friends and some of those relationships will never go away. I'm sure of that.

This cast of characters includes from left to right, Rob Sandler, Mark Weiner, Bob Nathan, Al Goldberg, me, Al Symkus and Harvey Zack.

The picture on the previous page was taken at Plainridge Park Casino in Plainridge, MA. Nothing like taking a short trip to watch NFL football games on a Sunday, surrounded by plenty of big screen TV's. The beer goes down easier when you're surrounded by friends, playing some keno and at half-time trying your luck at the tables.

Another "friends" group is my poker buddies. We've been playing poker since 1983. The games aren't as frequent, normally 3-4 times per year, but the get-togethers are something to look forward to. The group includes my brother Ken, the Kirkland brothers Bruce and Scott, Mitch Fishman, Scott Cohen, Paul Richmond and Mitch Karman. At the end of each game, we keep track of everyone's wins and losses. Then, when the year comes to an end, the person who has won the most money is declared the "Poker Player of the Year." At the first game of the next year, that person is awarded a plaque with their named engraved next to the other yearly winners. Don't know anybody that does that either. Call us crazy, but the money is still secondary to the friendships. In fact, I feel pretty bad when someone loses more than their fair share. What games do we play, you ask? Five and seven card stud, five-card poker, a crazy game called "guts" and a few hands of Texas hold'em.

Priceless reunion pic with the Bahn's, Frank's and Yanofsky's. Do I look anything like the actor Milo Ventimiglia from 'This is Us?'

Viva Las Vegas with the Zacks.

Sunset Cruise in FL. We like the mixed fruity beverages.

Four of us in Vegas, those drinks were deadly but oh so good!

Fashionable Mark Weiner at the Patriots Pro Shop.

The Three Musketeers, Mike, me and Roger.

238

Mark and Daniel share stories about their favorite all-time concerts.

Toga Party with our Nashua, NH neighbors, it was a three-hour tour, no correct that, it was a 10-day cruise.

Daniel and me at my 50th and in the middle is the talented and loveable Mark Hobbs.

AFC Championship Get-Together, Patriots win again!

Then, there's my biking buddies. I've been riding my hybrid bike for a while, but over the past year, it's my number one source of exercise. I have found some beautiful bike trails nearby and on most nice days, put the bike on the rack, head to the trail, put on my special ear piece for music on my I-phone and ride. The Bruce Freeman Trail begins in Chelmsford. There's a new trail in Salem, New Hampshire that's fantastic. Also worth mentioning is the Minuteman Trail in Lexington and of course maybe the best of the rest, the Cape Cod trail. I normally do ten miles in one hour. Not that far, not that long, but for me I certainly feel a sense of accomplishment.

Me and Harvey biking in Sarasota, Florida

Richard and me in Salem, NH, two dads putting up impressive miles!

CHAPTER NINETEEN

Tribute to Bernie

Stairway to Heaven by Daniel Yanofsky

Five AM is not a time typically seen by a high school student in the middle of the school year. However, I was up one morning at 5:00 AM. That was the day of the annual school talent show, and I would be performing in it that night. I was also performing before school started to a crowd of whoever would stop and listen on the way to their lockers. However, that was not all that would happen that day.

I remember so vividly walking into my parent's room to wake my dad up so that he could drive me and hearing the phone ring. To this day, I cannot forget the way my mom, through tears said, "Is he gone?" She was talking to my grandmother, who had received word from the doctor that my grandfather's passing was imminent. My grandfather had suffered from lung cancer and the chemotherapy treatment had put him in a grave condition. He was not strong enough to hold on.

My dad drove me in and my band played to the students coming into school. That was one of the longest school days I can remember. I could hardly focus that day. I had never had anyone that close to me die. I didn't know what to do. I hardly spoke. I barely ate. The people around me could tell something was wrong. One of my friends came up to me and asked, "girl trouble?" I solemnly shook my head. When the bell finally rang at the end of school, I ran to the closest spot I could find that my stubborn cell phone could hold on to a signal. With my girlfriend holding my hand, my dad told me that my grandfather had died. He had held on long enough for my mom, my dad, my aunt and my grandmother to be with him as he passed. They watched as the blips of his heartbeat on the ECG slowly stopped. He told me they would be back later, so I stayed in the comfort of my girlfriend and my friends for the afternoon.

I called my dad after I had eaten some dinner, and asked him what I should do about the show. He told me to play because both he and I knew that my grandpa would have wanted me to. My grandfather never wanted anyone making a fuss about him, even when he was at his worst. So, I returned to the school. It hurt to know that I wasn't there with my family when he passed and that I never got to say goodbye to him. It was then that I realized I could say goodbye, in my own special way, through song. While backstage with my group, a thought had occurred to me. Our band was slated to close the show with a performance of Led Zeppelin's "Stairway to Heaven." I knew at that very moment, my grandfather could be walking the stairway himself. So, I had a conference with my band and we decided that it would be appropriate to dedicate the song to him.

When our band came on stage, I walked out to the front of the stage and addressed the audience. I thanked them for coming and told them that we would be playing as people left the show. I then told them about my grandfather and how this song would be for him.

Nobody left.

As we played, I saw him in my mind. That might have been the reason I accidentally went into the last verse four measures early, but I recovered. I just hoped that our song would reach him. I put my heart into my drumsticks as we came into the coda. With the final lyric lingering in the auditorium, the crowd got to their feet in thunderous applause. I knew that if my grandfather had been there, he would have been on his feet as well.

CHAPTER TWENTY

List of Favorites

This is sort of a fun list to compile. Maybe it would serve well as an interesting Facebook poll. We may have more in common with each other than we thought!

Favorite Guilty pleasure—food: Mocha Chip Ice Cream in a waffle cone

Favorite Sports to Play: Basketball, billiards, wallyball (familiar with that one?), Cycling

Favorite performers: The Beatles, Frank Sinatra, Queen, the Doors, the Temptations, Chicago

Favorite all-time athletes: John Havlicek, Willie Mays, Larry Bird, Bill Russell, Tom Brady

Favorite sports writers: Jackie MacMullan, Bob Ryan and Dan Shaughnessy

Favorite "last meal": BBQ chicken with ribs, steak fries and corn on the cob

Favorite vacation spot: Siesta Key in Sarasota, Florida and Las Vegas, I was going to say Revere Beach but the pigeons got in the way

Favorite Italian restaurant: Javelli's in East Boston. The European in the North End was outstanding before they closed

Favorite Steak house: Abe and Louie's with the Capital Grille not too far behind

Favorite feel good songs: (I love music so there's plenty of favs. Here's just a few)

"Maybe I'm Amazed" by McCartney, "Make Me Smile" by Chicago, "You Make Me Feel So Young" by Sinatra, "Bohemian Rhapsody" and "Under Pressure" by Queen, "Carry On" by Crosby, Stills, Nash and Young, "Don't Stop Believin'" by Journey

Favorite Female Singers: Barbra Streisand, Aretha Franklin, Ella Fitzgerald

Favorite Male Singers: Frank Sinatra, Paul McCartney, John Lennon, Bobby Darin, Sammy Davis, Jr.

Favorite Actor: James Caan

Favorite Movie: Woody Allen's *Annie Hall*

Favorite Sports Rivalries: Red Sox-Yankees and Celtics-Lakers

Favorite Broadway Musicals: *Fiddler on the Roof, West Side Story*

Final question of the day...

If you were able to go out to dinner with any celebrity dead or alive, who would it be?

Easy... Frank Sinatra, Paul McCartney, Martin Luther King and Barbra Streisand

CHAPTER TWENTY-ONE

In Memoriam

"It's hard to forget someone who gave me so much to remember... I thought that we would have more time."

WKBR 1250 am/Manchester. N.H.
Al Blake, Jr.
Introduced me to the Queen City. Personable and caring, Al had become a good friend of mine during my tenure at WKBR. Al was a great family man and possessed a huge heart every day of his life.

Charlie Dent, Jr.
I worked with him at three different radio stations. Charlie succeeded in radio sales and management and later would own his own advertising agency. He was also an accomplished musician. I looked at Charlie as my mentor in those days and got the chance to tell him so a few days before his death.

WCGY/WCCM…Lawrence, Ma
Bruce Arnold Salvucci

Bruce was the glue and the driving force of one of my all-time radio families. Known as "Mr. Radio," Bruce spent 50-plus years as the mainstay of radio broadcasting in the Merrimack Valley. He was a true professional and incredible human being who taught me so much about being a manager and a human being. Bruce served as an inspiration to us all.

John Bassett

I considered Bruce Arnold and John Bassett as my second and third fathers. 'JB' served as general manager at WCCM and was Curt Gowdy's right hand man. It was so easy to talk to this man. He was a sports geek like me and we really clicked from the first day I met him. I miss our conversations very much.

Gene Silver

The matriarch of the WCGY/WCCM family and everyone's "second" mother. She was tough, intelligent and a sweetheart all rolled up into one very special lady. She worked for the Gowdys for many years and kept the office and the business in perfect shape. Her office door was always open even when it was closed. I miss her spunk and caring nature very much.

WXRV/92.5 the River, Haverhill, Mass
Steve Adolphson

The quintessential gentlemen, Steve worked for the River for 27 years and was certainly the right hand man for its owner, Steven Silberberg, during that time period. Mild-mannered, caring and a great listener was just some of his incredible attributes. Our time working together was very special and the devotion he had for the radio station and its owner was never-ending. He was simply the best form of humankind that you can ever imagine.

Adrienne Montezinos

I worked with Adrienne for four years. It was her first radio sales position and she made her mark in the industry in a very short time. Adrienne was very intelligent and an incredible writer. She was an accomplished dancer and actress and had a huge zest for life, not to mention an infectious laugh. Adrienne was taken from us far too early and I miss her and the good times that we shared.

Steven Silberberg

Steven was the owner of the River. I worked alongside him for 14 memorable years. He passed away suddenly in early 2021 and we were all shocked. I wish I had the chance to speak with him one last time. Steven was unique in his approach for sure, but had a sincere and dedicated love for his family as well as his radio family. A love that will forever be etched in his legacy. Steven also had a deep love for his farm in Bedford, NH. That was his escape from the crazy world of radio and it undoubtedly held a special spot in his heart. He gave me the support to succeed in management, but more importantly we shared some very special moments and I will always miss him.

Mark Hatem

A friend of mine who worked in the broadcast industry for many years. He passed away in March 2021 due to COVID-19. Mark was in his early 60's. I saw him at my retirement party a couple of years ago. He was a hard-working guy who cared very much about the people around him. An extremely nice guy who will missed by many.

CHAPTER TWENTY-TWO

Saving the Best for Last

In September of 2021, Paula and I will be celebrating our 40th wedding anniversary! That's 14,600 days being married to this tremendous woman. I kid around when I say that I must've been quite a salesman. After all, I sold Paula on marrying me! She's beautiful inside and out and is an incredible wife, mother and friend. She has a heart of gold and I've been the luckiest man on the planet to be able to call her my wife.

Add to that, she's also one heckuva cook. One only needs to look at me and see that I continue to bulge at the equator (i.e. my stomach). In retirement, our passions are long walks on the beach and romantic evenings watching *This is Us,* or binge-watching a number of Netflix series. Of course, getting together with family or friends or both tops the list.

Another admirable quality of my wife is her kind heart and consideration of others around her. Most notably her dedication to my 90-year old mother. She treats her as if my mother was her mother. Always by my side taking care of mother's every whim. Believe me, sometimes it isn't easy. Paula was also there with me during my dad's final days in the hospital. Supportive, loving and caring. That's Paula.

Hanging out in Newton.

Another successful puzzle completed!

I know I'm getting overly mushy, but I can't believe that she has stuck with me for 40 years! Truly amazing! Actually to make it official, September 6, 2021 marks the big 4-0, known as the "ruby" anniversary. She deserves more than a small chapter in this book, but then again she'd be embarrassed if I continued to lavish praise upon her.

I love you Paula.

CHAPTER TWENTY THREE

Parting Shots

I thought of several different ways to close this book and even how to title this chapter.

It could have been "Final Thoughts," (Jerry Springer?) "Never Can Say Good-bye," (Jackson Five) "In the End" (Beatles), "Dream On" (Aerosmith), "Parting Shots" or "The Best is Yet to Come" (Sinatra). So, as you can see the winner ended up being "Parting Shots," not a song at all.

Why "Parting Shots" you ask? There was a very popular sports television program on ESPN called the *Sports Reporters*. It was a round table discussion including some of the most prominent sportswriters in the country. The show first aired in 1988 and lasted nearly 30 years. To me, it was must-see TV, airing every Sunday morning at 9:30am. At the conclusion of each show, the panelists would give their "parting shots," a brief commentary on a chosen sports topic. Today, the show has been re-created as a podcast twice a week with three very talented sportswriters who were also on the TV version: Bob Ryan, Mike Lupica and Mitch Albom. As I said it was must-see TV, now it's must-listen to radio. Smart, quick-witted and knowledgeable about the world of sports and life in general. All three are award-winning authors. Thus, in my round about way, that's the name of this chapter.

This chapter will be a mish-mash of favorite quotes, life philosophies and a little bit more.

First, a word about my new lifestyle called retirement. In a book called *How to Retire Happy, Wild, and Free*, the author Ernie J. Zelinski stated….

"You have attained true freedom in this world when you can get up in the morning when you want to get up, go to sleep when you want to go to sleep and in the interval, work and play at the things you want to work and play at---all at your own pace. The great news is that retirement allows you the opportunity to attain this freedom."

As much as this quote hits the nail on the head and life as a retiree comes with all the above benefits, there are still times when I miss the social aspect of working. Those 41 years in radio meant hundreds of co-workers and clients, all very unique and special in their own ways. In retirement, you tend to question your own self-worth, your purpose in life or the thought when I wake up each day, does anybody really need me? I guess that's a natural thought process for any retiree. Radio was truly a blast. Whether it was station events, concerts, company softball games, lunches with co-workers or after hour drinks, there was always something going on. So, does retirement mean that the party is over? With your former co-workers, does it mean, out of sight, out of mind?

When I retired in 2018, I did think that was the case, but after further review the answer is simple. You make adjustments as you enter the next chapter in your life. It's imperative that you form your own personal game plan. You establish goals, just like in sales. You then execute that game plan to achieve a most satisfying life style; one that gives you a feeling of accomplishment. For me, I cycle as much as possible for exercising my body and my mind. I work around the house more often, something I never had much time doing while being in the work force. I spend more time with my wife, which is a very good thing. In fact, I appreciate her more than ever. I look forward to seeing Daniel, his wife, Merry and her parents, Linda and Richard, to plan our next dinner, BBQ or trip together.

It will be a lot of fun again to see my former co-workers. It will be even more special when we meet since I no longer see them five days a week at work. Weekend get-togethers with friends certainly make Paula and I happy. Of course during the year 2020, there was a horrible pandemic. Wearing masks and social distancing was the new norm. Social interaction went out the door as we suddenly faced some serious challenges.

I am hopeful that very soon and for everyone's sake, life will return to normalcy.

This chapter could be looked upon as a compilation of my thoughts, what I've learned about life and what I'd like to share with you as my "parting shots" before my first book comes to an end.

Time for some of my most favorite quotes. The first one is not really a quote but lines from a very cool song that came out in 1970. "Everybody is a Star" by Sly and the Family Stone.

"Everybody is a star, I can tell the way you shine on me. I love you for who you are, not the one you feel you need to be."

OK, I wouldn't call this an inspirational quote, but one that gives me a little bit of a chuckle. A quote from comedian Steven Wright...

"If at first you don't succeed, then skydiving definitely isn't for you."

I've learned that not everyone is going to like you, even though some pretend to for their own personal gains. That's OK and there's only one way to look at it with this quote.

"Don't worry about the people in your past. There's a reason they didn't make it to your future." Author unknown

And here's an important life lesson quote...

"There comes a time in your life, when you walk away from all the drama and people who create it. You surround yourself with people who make you laugh. Forget the bad and focus on the good. Love the people who treat you right, pray for the ones who do not. Life is too short to be anything but happy. Falling down is a part of life, getting back up is living." -- Jose N. Harris

And here's two quotes from someone very famous in my life.

"Treat people the way you want to be treated."

"It doesn't cost any more to be nice to people."

My mother, Jackie

This book started out as a chapter by chapter re-cap of my seven "radio" families and the people who influenced my life. I ended up filling in the blanks with childhood moments that led up to my radio career. Then, I felt the need to include my family and friends through words and pictures. No, that still wasn't enough for me. Being a sports fanatic, I wanted to share some of the unique stories that I experienced along the way. Then, while I'm at it, why not share some of my poetry. Little did I know that I would be writing a book that would contain 40,000 words. As I said previously, this book was a dream come true. My life was a dream come true and all of you that made it through these many pages played a part in inspiring me to keep writing because in the end, I guess I really did have a lot to say.

Thank you. I love you all. Be happy and always remember, treat people the way you'd like to be treated. The world will be a better place.

Steve (Young) Yanofsky

YOUNG AT HEART

Fairy tales can come true

It can happen to you, if you're young at heart.

For it's hard, you will find to be narrow of mind if you're young at heart.

You can go to extremes with impossible schemes,

You can laugh when your dreams fall apart at the seams.

And life gets more exciting with each passing day,

And love is either in your heart or on its way.

Don't you know that it's worth every treasure on earth to be young at heart.

For as rich as you are, it's much better by far to be young at heart.

And if you should survive to a hundred and five, look at all you'll derive out of being alive.

And here is the best part, you have a head start, if you are among the very young at heart.